Human Rights

– Illusory Freedom

Human Rights

– Illusory Freedom

Luke Gittos

Winchester, UK
Washington, USA

First published by Zero Books, 2019
Zero Books is an imprint of John Hunt Publishing Ltd., No. 3 East St., Alresford,
Hampshire SO24 9EE, UK
office1@jhpbooks.net
www.johnhuntpublishing.com
www.zero-books.net

For distributor details and how to order please visit the 'Ordering' section on our website.

ISBN: 978 1 78535 687 2
978 1 78535 688 9 (ebook)
Library of Congress Control Number: 2017962512

A CIP catalogue record for this book is available from the British Library.

Design: Stuart Davies

Printed and bound by CPI Group (UK) Ltd, Croydon, CR0 4YY, UK

We operate a distinctive and ethical publishing philosophy in
all areas of our business, from our global network of authors to
production and worldwide distribution.

Contents

Introduction

In the course of writing this book, the UK was subject to three terrorist attacks in Westminster, Manchester and London Bridge. These followed two previous incidents of Islamist terror against the United Kingdom. The first involved the bombing of the London underground by Islamist terrorists in 2005 and the second involved the stabbing of Fusilier Lee Rigby outside his barracks in Woolwich during 2013.

These attacks took place alongside interminable debate about the Human Rights Act. The vote for Brexit in June 2016 raised new questions about whether we should remain under the jurisdiction of the European Court of Human Rights (ECtHR). The Court in Strasbourg, which passes human rights judgements which must be taken into account by our Courts, had been blamed in the popular press for holding up the deportation of terror suspects. Critics of the Court said in August 2015 that the Court was 'spiralling out of control' after it was revealed that among the 94 successful claimants to the Court since 1975 were included convicted murderers, IRA gunmen and suspects linked to Islamist terror. It was thought, in the aftermath of the Brexit vote, that the Tories may have had a sufficient mandate to finally repeal the Human Rights Act, something that they had promised to do since 2005[1]. Then, following a disastrous election result in 2017, in which Theresa May lost her overall majority, a weakened Tory party looked unlikely to repeal the Act before the 2022 election at the very least.

The starting point of this book is that our debate about Human Rights is so interminable, so marred in misinformation, because we are failing to properly address some of the key legal and moral questions of our time. Complex legal and moral questions are now left to Judges to decide, where the political and moral debates around them have been exhausted. Because

1

we are unable to formulate a common political response to the questions raised by human rights cases, we become dependent on an unaccountable Judiciary to provide answers. This means both sides become entrenched. Human Rights proponents point to individual cases with apparently progressive results to make an argument that the Human Rights Act is a vital defender of the most vulnerable. Individual stories about the impact of the Act work to portray it as having a unique power to introduce compassion into our Court system. Human Rights detractors use broad and inaccurate statistics to suggest that the Human Rights Act prevents justice being delivered against the most serious criminals. Both of these approaches obscure the reality about what is at stake.

The Human Rights Act has passed significant control to judges to adjudicate over important questions regarding our political freedom. It has developed the political role of the Judiciary and granted them a greater say over significant matters in public life. It is this development that we should be discussing. This cannot afford to be a narrow, legalistic discussion. We cannot avoid the new circumstances that we face around the threat of nihilistic Islamist violence both at home and abroad. Rather than becoming unduly fearful about repealing the Human Rights Act, we should start by taking an objective look at how the Judiciary has purported to protect important political freedoms in the 17 years since the Act was passed. This book is a short contribution to this discussion.

We should remember that the left has traditionally been sceptical about the power of Judges to help safeguard freedom. My argument is that withdrawing the mechanism through which the Judiciary control our civil liberties would not immediately lead to a loss of freedom. In fact, our fear in the face of the arguments for repeal show how dependent we have become on the law and the Judiciary to answer the complex moral questions thrown up by contemporary life. This is not good for progressive, freedom orientated politics. We have nothing to fear from repealing the Human Rights Act if we are better equipped for the fight for civil liberty. This book is a short contribution to that fight.

Civil liberties in the UK

On Christmas Eve 2016, Munir Hassan Mohammed, 35, and Rowaida El-Hassan, 32 appeared at Westminster Magistrates' Court. They were charged with offences relating to obtaining chemicals for use in explosions as prohibited by the Terrorism Act of 2000. Two others appeared alongside them charged with preparing acts of terrorism. News of the arrests and the Court appearances made the BBC morning news. The reporting of the hearing was unremarkable. A date was set for the case to be heard at the Old Bailey and the group were remanded in custody[2].

Many listening would no doubt have greeted the story with relief. The plot had involved the detonation of a bomb using a mobile phone in the lead up to Christmas. El -Hassan had allegedly owned a manual on how to make bombs that he had sent to other potential recruits. The group were also charged with being members of a proscribed organisation under the Terrorism Act for allegedly belonging to Islamic state. Few would be waking up on Christmas Eve with any sympathy for the plotters.

But something about this case made it the perfect starting point for a book about the state of human rights in the United Kingdom. In the final moments of the radio report the correspondent mentioned something that most people in the UK would simply no longer notice: the group had been held without charge for 12 days.

It's easy to ignore such an apparently trifling detail when the word 'terrorism' is mentioned. The hearing in London took place just weeks after Anis Amri drove a lorry into German citizens enjoying a Christmas market in Berlin and at the end of a year that had seen devastating terrorist atrocities in cities across

Europe. Between 2015 and 2017 similar attacks would strike cities across the continent, including London and Stockholm. The appalling attacks on the Bataclan and other sites across Paris were remarkable for their barbarity. The audience of that report could not have known that terror would strike in the UK throughout the year to come.

But it's also easy to forget that detention without charge was, for a long time, considered antithetical to the British idea of 'human rights'. The detention of these people for long periods of time, without providing sufficient evidence to charge them with a crime, would have been considered an affront to most common lawyers of the 19th Century.

Indeed, the first human rights to enter British law related to the ability for the authorities to detain people without good cause. When the barons petitioned King John in the 13th Century to recognise certain fundamental rights of his subjects, in a document that came to be known as 'Magna Carta', they stated: "No freeman shall be taken or imprisoned or disseised or exiled or in any way destroyed, nor will we go upon him nor will we send upon him except upon the lawful judgement of his peers or the law of the land." The charter enshrined the concept of Habeas Corpus into English jurisprudence. Translated as 'produce the body', Habeas Corpus recognised that citizens should not be imprisoned unless evidence could be brought to justify their detention. Of course, the 13th Century document did not do much to guarantee people's actual rights and people were often imprisoned arbitrarily in the centuries to come. But the ancient acknowledgement that the power of the king should – in principle – be limited by the evidence that existed against an accused laid the foundations for a British belief in the liberty of the person that would come to be central in our legal system in the centuries that followed.

The 20th Century was not kind to detention without charge. Both World War 1 and 2 saw radical limitations placed on the rights of citizens thought to be collaborating with the enemy. The Defence of the Realm Act 1914 meant the home secretary could intern people of German descent and was later used against Irish citizens suspected of involvement in the Easter Uprising. Colonial subjects were routinely detained without charge, most notoriously during the suppression of the armed Mau Mau uprising in Kenya[3], during which up to 60,000 Kikuyu were detained without any evidence against them. While detention without charge truly ended at the end of the 20th Century, in the course of New Labour's response to 9.11, it had been dying for many decades before that.

Detention without charge is not the only human right to have felt the impact of recent history. The Terrorism Act introduced a range of offences that directly targeted people's ability to say what they think and associate with who they chose. The Act outlawed inciting support for a 'proscribed organisation'. Organisations like the Kurdish PKK, who were fighting ISIS with increasing success in Northern Iraq, were banned from receiving any support from any British citizen. In 2016, the minute and inconsequential far right group National Action were proscribed as a terrorist organisation under the Act, meaning that they too could not be lawfully promoted in the UK. Before that, the nefarious and vague offence of 'glorifying terrorism' was used to target those demonstrating support for banned organisations. The UK government's 'Prevent' programme, which sought to intervene where young people were perceived to be at 'risk of radicalisation' has come under significant attack for apparently outlawing certain beliefs among the Muslim population. Our anti-terror regime has precipitated significant erosions of significant democratic freedoms.

However, you do not have to be a suspected terrorist to feel your freedom being undermined in contemporary Britain. Football fans in Scotland have been prosecuted for singing offensive songs. Tweeters have been thrown in jail for tweeting remarks at celebrities. Christian bakers have been successfully sued for refusing to bake a cake in support of gay marriage, a move that many thought undermined their freedom of conscience. People's private lives continue to be invaded relentlessly by a variety of organisations, from local authorities to the International intelligence services. We live in a country where our freedom to think, speak and believe what we choose is being eroded year on year.

Often these attacks on individual freedom are not very high profile. Many attacks on freedom occur in Magistrates' Courts up and down the country, in cases which are never reported in the newspapers. Community Protection Notices, introduced in 2014, allow for people to be fined and subsequently prosecuted for any behaviour that has a 'detrimental effect of a persisting and continuing nature on the quality of life of those in the locality'. CPNs have been used to justify wide ranging restrictions on what people say and do in the privacy of their homes. Human rights law does nothing to defend against this increasingly arbitrary interference by the state in people's lives.

Then take the presumption of innocence. In the 18th Century, the English Jurist William Blackstone famously proclaimed that it was better to let 100 guilty men go free than to allow one innocent to suffer. In recent years, the idea that people are innocent until proven guilty has faced significant challenges, both in law and in the public realm. Most recently, allegations of sexual misconduct have resulted in people losing their jobs and their livelihoods without ever facing a Court of law. The #Metoo movement, which seeks to publicly call out those accused of sexual misconduct, presents a challenge to the notion of presumed innocence, by calling for people to be 'punished' without ever having to formally adjudicate over a complaint. These violations of what once constituted important freedoms under English law are cheer-led by the political and media establishment. It seems some 'human rights violations' are more palatable for them than others.

We will see later in this book that other freedoms that we may once have thought of as human rights have been significantly eroded. Both Labour and Tory governments have contributed to the erosion of the right to silence, so that now juries are permitted to draw adverse inferences from a refusal of a criminal defendant to account for themselves. The Tory government pioneered a new disclosure regime in criminal cases which required a defendant to disclose the vast extent of their defence in a particular case in advance, so that the prosecution could no longer be ambushed by a defence case.

Much of this has been driven by people purportedly on the left. Consider the following facts. The New Labour government, which governed Britain between 1997 and 2005, were responsible for introducing both the Human Rights Act of 1998 and the provisions which allow for extensive detention without charge. The same government that introduced the Human Rights Act repealed the double jeopardy rule, which prevented people being prosecuted for the same crime twice. The same government that introduced the Human Rights Act also introduced the Regulation of Investigatory Powers Act 2002, a piece of law which is widely considered to be the greatest intrusion by the state into our private lives of modern times. The same government that introduced the Human Rights Act also introduced extensive laws regulating the use of speech and freedom of expression. Rather than give rise to a period of unbridled freedom, the introduction of the Human Rights Act was the prelude to the most draconian, anti-freedom period of law making in recent history[4].

So what should we think now, in 2017, when the Tory government plans to scrap the Act? For supporters of human rights laws, they represent the outcome of centuries of struggle against despotism and tyranny. They allow a basic respect for human dignity to permeate our legal system. Although many human rights supporters see problems with how the Human

Rights Act is applied, they also see our current framework as an incomplete project. It represents a small – but significant – step towards realising a universal respect for human dignity. For human rights proponents, attempts by a Tory government to repeal the Act represent part of an ongoing assault on liberal values, and an underhand attempt to invade more areas of our lives with state control.

For their detractors, human rights laws represent a judicially imposed curtailment on national sovereignty. They are an elite, judicial licence to control the parameters of our freedom. They allow for criminals to make a mockery of the justice system and for illegal immigrants to make a mockery of our border controls. Depending on who you speak to, human rights are either the high point of human rationality or the low point of liberal emotionalism.

This book does not argue any of the above. It does not indulge in hyperbolic rhetoric about what the Human Rights Act does nor does it pretend that repeal of the Act would be catastrophic. Instead, it argues that our fixation on human rights as guarantor for freedom is at best an equivocation. It argues that anyone who genuinely believes in freedom, progress and enlightened laws has nothing to fear from the repeal of the Human Rights Act. Firstly, because it simply is not that powerful. It does not prevent the government passing bad and draconian laws. But secondly, because I believe the existence of the Human Rights Act actively contributes to the erosion of civil liberties. Freedom has to be constantly fought for. The modern age presents us with many challenges to our principles. New moral questions raised by, for example, ISIS fighters returning from abroad have to be dealt with in the political realm, not in the Courtroom. The views of the public are vital to settling the complex moral questions of our age. Once we come to rely on the law to tell us how free we can be, we are no longer free at all. The argument of this book is that a respect for important freedoms among the public is the only dependable defence against increases in state power.

This is why human rights grant an illusory freedom. The illusion is that being compliant with human rights laws makes us free. The illusion is that this standard provides a guarantee for a meaningfully free society. This is why no liberal should fear the end of human rights laws. They are a shill. They have presided over the undermining and erosion of a number of significant democratic freedoms. This book argues that we should use the prospect of repeal not as an existential threat to freedom, but rather as an opportunity for its reaffirmation.

2016: Annus hornbills

Recent history suggests even the Human Rights Act's biggest detractors are scared of repealing it. The Tories had promised to repeal the Act within 100 days of their 2015 electoral victory. Michael Gove, the then justice secretary charged with delivering the repeal, said before a select committee that the repeal would happen in 'late 2016'. Commentators observed that Gove, in being appointed Justice Secretary, had been handed an impossible task of repealing the Human Rights Act within 100 days of a Conservative victory.

Repeal raised difficult questions about the constitutional implications for devolved parliaments in Wales and Scotland and Northern Ireland, which would be more likely to take 6 months to resolve rather than 100 days. It was not clear whether consent from devolved parliaments was required to repeal the Act or whether repeal would have an impact on the status of the Good Friday agreement. Before the select committee, Gove was chastised for enacting significant constitutional change for no good reason. The constitutional implications for the repeal meant that it would cause a significant level of disruption and require a significant amount of legislating, for very little practical purpose, given that the protections provided by the Human Rights Act would almost certainly have to be included in any new British Bill of Rights.

Then came the vote for Brexit. On 23 June 2016, 17.5 million people voted to leave the European Union. The feeling of shocked disbelief among members of the establishment was palpable. The vote had been in spite of a small army of experts warning of the dangers of leaving. David Cameron resigned, Theresa May took over as Prime Minister. It became a cliché to point out that the vote had sent 'shock waves' through the British establishment. Significantly, for the purposes of Human Rights repeal, Michael Gove lost his job as Justice Secretary to Liz Truss. The minister who had been charged with repealing the Act in the immediate aftermath of the election had been relegated to the backbenches.

In the weeks after the vote, it was thought that the Tories' plan to replace the Human Rights Act with a British Bill of Rights would be considered low priority. Truss was not considered sufficiently experienced to undertake a significant constitutional shift. The vote had arguably placated the right wing Tory backbenchers who were calling for the Human Rights Act to be repealed. Reports emerged that Theresa May had indicated in private that she 'might junk' the plan to repeal. However, newly incumbent justice secretary Liz Truss surprised most commentators in August 2016 when she indicated that she remained committed to withdrawal and was 'looking at the detail'.

Theresa May then announced, over Christmas 2016, that the Tories would fight the 2020 election on a pledge to repeal the Human Rights Act. It was nonetheless quite remarkable that the Prime Minster was willing to state that a promise that had appeared in a 2005 manifesto would also appear in their manifesto 15 years later, as though this represented a solid commitment to repeal.

The aftermath of the Brexit vote led many to see the anticipated repeal of the Human Rights Act as part of a broader retreat from cosmopolitanism and decency. It was as though we were entering a new era of British politics, characterised by parochialism and xenophobia[5]. The hostility to the European Court of Human Rights fitted into a narrative in which the Conservative party, enjoying a significant majority and an almost non-existent (at that stage) opposition under Jeremy Corbyn, were seeking to shut down all connections with our purportedly liberal past. The repeal of the Human Rights Act was just part of a broader collapse of liberal decency. It was the legal symbol of the end of the liberal era.

The hysteria was encouraged by supporters of the Act. When Liberty appointed a new director in June 2016, she remarked that the protection of the Human Rights Act was likely to be the 'struggle of our generation'. The website of Liberty claimed that repealing the Human Rights Act would 'weaken everyone's rights – leaving politicians to decide when our fundamental freedoms should apply'. One commentator suggested that repeal of the 1998 Act would take us back to a 'perceived idyll of the 1930s' that would leave its citizens 'deprived of rights or the means to enforce them before the Courts[6].' Another said that repeal would mean the UK state could 'pick and choose which rights it granted, much like Russia'. The idea that human rights repeal would propel us back into an age of apparent despotism was increasingly common among those who objected to repeal.

The apparent impact of repeal could even go well beyond the rights of the Act itself. In 2015, leading campaign group Amnesty International sent letters to Prime Minister David Cameron and Irish Taoiseach Enda Kenny warning that repealing the Human Rights Act could threaten peace in Northern Ireland, by undermining trust in the Irish police forces. For those like Liberty and Amnesty International who promote the cause of Human Rights, the repeal of the Human Rights Act is often presented as having catastrophic implications extending way beyond the legal remit of the Act itself.

What does the Human Rights Act do?

The Human Rights Act European incorporated the European Convention on Human Rights into the Law of the United Kingdom. This meant that people could enforce the rights contained under the convention in British Courts. It's important to note, in light of the mania induced by the prospect of repeal, that before 1998 when the Act was passed, the UK was already bound in law to observe the Convention following its ratification by the UK in 1951. UK citizens were able to petition their cases directly in the hope of receiving a remedy following any breach of their convention rights.

What the Human Rights Act did was make these rights enforceable in UK Courts. While Amnesty International claim that this 'sped up' the process of having rights enforced, it only did so because the rights were brought into the remit of the UK system. It certainly did not speed up the glacial pace of the European Court of Human Rights in disposing of cases.

Nonetheless, the Act was billed as a significant change to our legal system. New Labour introduced the Act as part of a broader programme of 'constitutional reform' which promised to renegotiate the relationship between the citizen and the state. This programme included the removal of the House of Lords from the houses of parliament, the introduction of elected peers into the House and the creation of the Supreme Court.

Section 2 of the Act said that any Court in England and Wales resolving a question regarding convention rights 'must take into account any (a) judgment, decision, declaration or advisory opinion of the European Court of Human Rights ... whenever made or given, so far as, in the opinion of the court or tribunal, it is relevant to the proceedings in which that question has arisen.'. British Judges are not 'bound' by European law, but in the early days of the Act the influence of Strasbourg jurisprudence was strong. From 2000 – 2009, 'the English Courts tended to follow Strasbourg jurisprudence as if it were a superior court in human rights law'. However, this changed. From 2009 onwards, Judges became more assertive about British jurisprudence. The influence of Strasbourg law has varied at various stages of the life of the Act.

Section 3 imposed an obligation on Judges in England to read and give effect to English law in accordance with convention rights, as 'far as it is possible to do so'. It was this section that gave the Act its first tests in the UK Courts. An early case involving the Act involved the House of Lords being asked to consider whether parliament's 'rape shield law', which prevented a defendant asking questions about a complainant's sexual history, violated Article 6 of the convention guaranteeing a right to a fair trial. Lord Steyn noted in his judgement that parliament had decided not to make the obligation to interpret if 'reasonable' do so. Instead, they had required to interpret 'as far as is possible to do so'. Accordingly, interpretation could be 'linguistically strained'[7]. Judges could read the law in a creative way in order to make it fit with the requirements of the convention.

Section 4 gave the Courts the power to issue a declaration of incompatibility in situations where law could not be read compatibly with the convention. There were many who, at the time that the law was being debated, wanted the new Human Rights Act to provide Courts with the power to strike down legislation that could not be read compatibly with the convention. The compromise was a declaration of incompatibility, which did not strike the law down, but sent it back to parliament with the implication that it would be amended[8]. The Courts proved willing to use their new remedy. Between 2000 and 2015, the Courts made 29 declarations of incompatibility. These included declarations with respect to the law regarding the disclosure of criminal convictions and police cautions and with regards to legislation relating to 'back to work schemes'. This section provided a route through which the judiciary could actively pass judgement on the legislating process.

Although the influence of Strasbourg cases waned towards the end of 2009, the initial effect of the Human Rights Act was a 'sea change' in judicial reasoning. Between 1975 and 1996, the jurisprudence of the European Court was considered in 316 cases in the English High Court. Between October 2000 and April 2002 the jurisprudence of the European Court was considered in 431 cases in the High court or above. It affected the outcome in 318 of those cases[9]. The influence of European law over the thinking of English Judges was immediate and remarkable.

The political Judiciary

One important dimension in the discussion of the virtues of the Act is the politicised judiciary. In 2016, when the UK Supreme Court decided that the Prime Minister Theresa May needed a parliamentary vote to trigger Article 50, thereby commencing the process of leaving the European union, the Daily Mail newspaper ran a headline with pictures of the Judges presiding with the headline 'enemies of the people'. There followed a fevered debate about the relationship of the Judiciary to politics. The then Justice Secretary Liz Truss was widely criticised by legal journalists for failing to defend the independence of the Judiciary. Members of Parliament from both sides of the debate criticised the headline, claiming that the decision represented an impartial assessment of ancient common law principles. Indeed, by the time the Supreme Court decision was announced, a vote in parliament had occurred and the final decision was largely academic. What remained, in the aftermath of that headline, was a lingering question about the Judiciary's apparent involvement in important political processes.

It's been 40 years since JAG Griffith made the point that our judiciary is inherently political. In his 1977 work the Politics of the Judiciary, which was deeply controversial at the time, Griffith pointed out that Judges could not help but make politicised decisions. They were part of the machinery of the state. In deciding the 'correct' way of interpreting a particular statute, they were developing or refining the meaning of the statute to accommodate particular facts. This process involved political judgements. What proved more controversial was Griffith's claim that 'people like members of the Judiciary, relatively homogenous in character are faced with (controversial cases), act in broadly similar ways...behind these actions lies a unified attitude of mind, one concerned with protecting and conserving certain values and institutions'. Griffith's claim, that the Judiciary was dominated by a conservative mind set, was controversial for the legal establishment who preferred to consider their Judges as entirely immune from political influence[10].

Griffith identified the changing role of the Judiciary, from neutral proclaimers of what the law was to a more positive law making role. He could not have predicted how that political role would expand in the decades to come. In 1999, developing Griffith's analysis, Kate Malleson identified what she termed the 'new Judiciary', a new kind of public body which fell between the explicit law making role of parliament and the old restricted role of the Judiciary as a neutral translator of the law. When Malleson was writing, the Judiciary had already transformed into a monitoring body for public policy. The number of Judges between 1970 and 1999 had more than doubled. There had been a significant growth of Judicial Review, with more and more ministerial decisions being subject to Judicial intervention. A civil service training document published in 1998 called '*A judge over your shoulder*' spoke to a new role for the Judiciary as a policy watchdog. Malleson also correctly identified the Human Rights Act as a precursor to a further expansion of the Judiciary's role in political life[11].

Because the Judiciary's political role is often exaggerated, it is important to be clear what we mean when we describe a 'political' Judiciary. Judges are not party political. They certainly do not wear their politics on their sleeve. In a recent documentary about the UK Supreme Court, Lord Kerr was dismissive of the idea that the Supreme Court judges were driven by politics. It is certainly the case that Judges routinely make decisions which are contrary to their political or personal wishes for the outcome of the case. Indeed, the scope for 'Judicial Activism' seems markedly narrower in the UK than in other jurisdictions. Our Judiciary has far more limited powers than the Judiciary does in the US, where legislation can be struck down by the Supreme Court if it conflicts with the constitution. Judges in the UK are unelected and so are not subject to the same pressures as some Judges in the Appellate Courts of the US.

Griffith said: 'political cases are those which arise out of controversial legislation... which touch on important moral or social issues'. This is part of the picture. But the position of the Judiciary today is affected not only by the cases brought before it. The political nature of our judiciary does not straightforwardly arise from direct activism of the Judiciary itself. Instead, it arises from the lack of authority in other important institutions of government. The ability of either individual minsters or political parties to command public confidence is at an all-time low. Contemporary political parties are unable to achieve the loyalty of a consistent voter base. Support for the two main parties ebbs and flows between various social groups. As the authority of politicians and political parties has waned, Judges have increasingly become vestiges of authority for political decision making. A decision or report of a Judge in a case or Judicial Inquiry is now a vital precursor to any significant political decision.

This is starkly illustrated by the rise and changing role of the public inquiry. The establishment of Public Inquiries at the start of the 20th Century was established in order to allow for objective investigations into parliamentary affairs in circumstances where the integrity of parliamentary officials had been called into question. Inquiries allowed for an objective third party to rule over a narrow set of facts to establish whether any wrong doing could be attributed to the organs of government. Today, such Inquiries have been charged with delivering historic judgements over the political decision making of the past. The decision to go to war in Iraq, the regulation of the media, the regulation of childcare have all been subject to extensive public inquiries which have cast verdicts over the propriety of individual decision makers. In a climate in which every political decision may be open to some kind of review, being backed up by a Judicial Report or decision lends valuable authority to the decisions of political actors.

It is in this context that we need to consider the Human Rights Act. The Act was an explicit mandate to the Judiciary to shape political freedom. It expanded the role of the judiciary in resolving fundamentally political issues. As we will see, the tests of the European Convention place Judges in the position of judging the effectiveness of particular policies and their impact on the society they are considering. We have to consider why it is that Judges have such a central role in deciding some of the key moral and political questions of our time.

Freedom without human rights

What is at stake in repealing the Human Rights Act is the Judiciary's ability to control the parameters of political freedom. Rather than become apoplectic at the prospect of repealing the Act, we should begin by considering whether the Judiciary is the proper institution for protecting our freedom.

The central argument is that human rights are a weak guarantee for freedom. Importantly, the solution is not more human rights laws. Instead, we need to begin by reconstituting a respect for political freedom among members of the public. If this is our starting point, we have nothing to lose from repealing the Human Rights Act. This book does not give a comprehensive account of what such freedom should look like.

Instead, it critiques the model of freedom offered up by human rights institutions. It is a polemic and so will inevitably fail to satisfy those who have devoted their careers to human rights jurisprudence. This may be no bad thing. If we are to rekindle the aspiration for freedom we need to start by looking beyond the Courts and beyond the legal establishment. But first we should consider how human rights came to be so central to our political and legal culture. For this, we need to consider the recent history of the Labour party and its political reorientation during the late 1980s and early 1990s. We will then consider how freedom should be discussed in the context of recent terror attacks, before considering in detail the confused and self-serving claims of the human rights industry. This will lead to a consideration of recent human rights jurisprudence and a critique of the qualified model of political freedom offered up by the judgements of our human rights Courts.

Human Rights and the Labour party

The left's embrace of human rights law is a historical peculiarity. Human rights in Europe were pioneered by conservatives who were concerned about the spread of socialism. They were formulated as a means of defending conservative, Christian values from the perceived threat of the Soviet Union. In the UK, the introduction of the Human Rights Act came about because of the historical weakness of the left within the Labour party and the reorientation of the party around a cosmopolitan, middle class voting base. The human rights framework was the brainchild of commercial lawyers at the head of the Labour party who had ascended as the left factions of the party had been retreating. The embrace of human rights by today's left is in spite of the fact that today's framework was dreamt up in opposition to socialism. It was a symptom of the collapse of the left, not of its ascendency.

Human rights and the fear of democracy

In the aftermath of the Brexit vote, supporters of human rights were keen to emphasise that leaving the EU did not mean leaving the remit of the European Court of Human Rights. Retaining the human rights regime came to be seen as retaining some vestige of the progressive European project. It was as though, in the aftermath of Brexit, 'all was not lost' as long as we held on to human rights laws. Human rights proponents were keen to highlight the fact that the Human Rights Act was passed by our own parliament and did not represent a law 'imposed by Brussels'. The fact that the Convention has been incorporated into English law is also used as a retort when the human rights regime is called 'undemocratic'.

Aspects of this are technically true. The EU and the European Court of Human Rights are legally separate institutions. The European Convention on Human Rights came into force in 1953 and Britain granted the individual right to petition the Court in 1966. The UK did not join the European Economic Community until 1976. The European convention is now a part of English law through the 1998 Human Rights Act, which was passed by our parliament under the leadership of Tony Blair. The presence of the Human Rights regime in UK law cannot be attributed to any foreign body nor is there anything to say that leaving the EU entails leaving the European Court of Human Rights.

However, it is also right to see the EU and the European Court of Human Rights as politically and historically aligned. Both the institutions of the EU and the European Court of Human Rights developed out of the emerging European movement following the Second World War. This movement was motivated by the need to manage democracy in the face of political threats to conservative ruling elites, specifically the perceived threat of the spread of socialism from Eastern Europe into the West[12].The existence of the human rights framework owes everything to attempts by post war elites to centralise economic and political control over the European continent and to manage the influence of the European public.

Until recently, the anti-democratic motivations of the Court's founders have been hidden by an appeal to humanitarian motivations. It has become commonly accepted that the creation of the European Court of Human Rights, and related human rights institutions, were designed to 'prevent a repeat of the atrocities of war'. However, it is more accurate to say that the 'atrocities or war' were used as a means of discrediting democracy as a means of protecting individual rights.

Marco Duranti's recent book *The Conservative Human Rights Revolution*, provides insight into the anti-democratic foundation of the European human rights movement. According to Duranti, the 'surprisingly small group of individuals (who) shaped the basic contours of the European human rights system', yearned for the mythical Christian Europe of a bygone age[13']. These were individuals like David Maxwell Fyfe, a staunch free market conservative. He, like Churchill, saw a serious threat in the apparently socially democratic direction taken by Britain following the election of Clement Atlee. Socialist and communist parties contributed to the drafting of the European Convention and there could be little doubt that the Convention had a 'socially democratic orientation', but the primary role of the human rights framework was to provide an alternative moral framework to that offered by socialism.

The European Human Rights movement began in 1948. World War 2 had concluded with the division of Berlin between East and West. The Soviet Union had blocked access to West Berlin in response to the Western allies introducing the Deutschemark. Also in that year, countries in both the East and the West of Europe began receiving 13 billion in aid from America under the Marshall Plan, which many saw as an attempt at suppressing Communist influence in Western Europe[14]. Perhaps most significantly, the Communist party of Czechoslovakia, backed by the Soviet Union, staged the 'Victorious February' Coup de tat – seizing power that they would retain for two decades. This represented the first overthrow of a democratic government by Soviet backed forces since the conclusion of the war. These events created an atmosphere in which the fear of communism among Europe's elites was at the forefront of foreign policy.

It was against this background that the first Hague conference took place. At the Hall of Knights, a network of politicians, journalists, philosophers, artists and thinkers gathered to discuss the future of Europe. The hall was a palatial banqueting space, which set the Congress up as an alternative parliament for a divided continent. 800 contributors attended at the invitation of the International Committee of the Movements for European Unity, an organisation which collated the various campaigns for increased European federalism which had persisted since the early 20th Century. Seventeen countries were represented. The purpose of the congress was to 'demonstrate the existence, in all free countries of Europe, of a body of public opinion in support of European unity, to discuss the challenges posed by European unity and propose practical solutions to governments'. By the end of the Congress, the delegates would have formulated a 'message to Europeans', promising the formulation of a new 'human rights court' and the establishment of United Europe, throughout whose area 'the free movement of persons, ideas and goods is restored'.

The reference to 'free' countries was highly significant. Firstly, because it defined those attending the congress in opposition to the unfree countries of Eastern Europe, who the West wanted to portray as beholden to Moscow. But secondly, because it showed how the Congress was setting about to define what it meant to be a 'free' country in post war Europe. To be 'free' meant to be free from communism. Right from its inception, the European movement attempted to take ownership of the meaning of freedom as part of its attempt to define itself against the evils of the Soviet Union. Human rights laws would come to be fundamental to the European movement's attempt to define freedom in its own image.

The men who arrived in the Hague intent on crafting a new future for Europe were, in Duranti's words, 'united in their belief that a democracy in which tyranny of the majority held sway was little better than a dictatorship'. Duranti notes 'while their socialist opponents called them anti-democratic, conservatives saw their aim at the Hague congress as protecting democracy from itself'. Throughout the Congress, the spectre of Nazism and the threat of communism were presented as possible outcomes to untrammelled democracy.

Winston Churchill opened proceedings at The Hague by proclaiming that the Congress could 'fairly claim to be the voice of Europe'. Without reading too much into Churchill's opening remarks, these few words were telling. Churchill's claim that the congress could be considered the 'voice of Europe' was made despite the fact that most of the attendees were not there on any democratic mandate. While some delegations included serving members of parliament, the Congress was predominantly attended by people who had either recently been rejected by their voting public or had never won a vote in their lives. Those delegations which did include elected members of parliament tended to be dominated by Catholic conservatives over liberals and socialists. The claim in the Congress' mission statement that they wished to 'demonstrate the existence, in all free countries of Europe, of a body of public opinion in support of European unity' suggested that the performative display of unity was more important than its political substance.

Churchill argued that nation state based democracy had been responsible for the rise of Hitler. He spoke of 'the gradual assumption by all the nations concerned of that larger sovereignty (as opposed to national sovereignty) which can alone protect their diverse and distinctive customs and characteristics and their national traditions all of which under totalitarian systems, whether Nazi, Fascist, or Communist, would certainly be blotted out for ever'. Throughout the Congress, totalitarianism would continue to be held up as a possible outcome for nation state democracy in Europe. Attendees talked about the need 'to modify the traditional nation state pattern, establish political jurisdiction broad enough to satisfy the political and economic needs' of the time. A speech given by one leader showed how human rights were always conceived of as part of broader efforts towards European feudalism. She proclaimed 'that (Europe's) future is a federalist future we believe that the defence of human rights is impossible in international terms except in a federalist framework'.

The threat of communism was key among the concerns for Churchill personally. He had written to Anthony Eden in 1942 to say that his "thoughts rest[ed] primarily in [. . .] the revival and glory of Europe," and feared that Europe's only other path was 'toward Bolshevism'. He had been ousted from the UK government in 1945 by Clement Atlee's Labour party on a programme of wide ranging social reform. The creation of the welfare state, the establishment of the National Health Service and a programme for mass home building had proved popular with the British public. Churchill had accused Atlee of attempting to install a 'socialist dictatorship' in Britain in the run up to the election. His address to the Congress regularly equated Communism with Nazism, saying 'Europe has only to arise and stand in her own majesty, faithfulness and virtue, to confront all forms of tyranny, ancient or modern, Nazi or Communist'.

Today, 'protecting democracy from itself' is still at the heart of the human rights movement. A 2017 report by a conservative think tank identifies the human rights act as a vital curb on the 'totalitarian' impulses of a socialist government under Jeremy Corbyn[15], on the basis that the Convention is deferential to private property rights. A 2017 campaign by the left leaning human rights group Rights Info crowd funded a film on how human rights can 'stop the rise of far-right'. The Crowdfunding invitation featured footage of Nazi parades and Jews in Auschwitz interspersed with modern footage of marches by the English Defence League and US white nationalists[16]. The message of the film was that human rights in the present can prevent the repeat of evils in the past, placing a curb on the apparent rise of the far right among the general population. The claim that democracy gives rise to tyranny has remained the central argument of human rights supporters from their inception to the modern day.

The fear of socialism motivated other Human Rights institutions as well. Kirsten Sellers' book *The Rise of Human Rights* explores in forensic detail how the Universal Declaration of Human Rights arose from the West's need to present a coherent self-image following the second world war, explaining how human rights went from a fringe interest among a minority of academic lawyers to 'formulating the language of late 20th Century international relations'. The shambolic and inconclusive trials at Nuremberg and Tokyo against war criminals symbolised a lack of moral authority experienced by the Allies in the aftermath of War. The language of 'human rights' moved from a fringe obsession among international lawyers to a key tool in the armoury of political actors precisely because universalism and consensus were missing from the conduct of international relations. In her words, "The iron fist of global power was thus wrapped in the velvet glove of international humanitarianism'.

For Sellers, ideas about Human Rights originated during the enlightenment, 'as reason began to triumph over religion and the new sensibility embraced ideals of individual freedom and social equality'. However, it was not until the early 1940s that the modern human rights system began to influence global politics. The human rights movement gained significant international momentum with the founding of the United Nations, in the San Francisco Conference in April 1945. America had laid the plans for a new 'international organisation' since before the war, one which would replace the precarious balance of power that had persisted in the early years of the 20th Century. This ‹new global conglomerate› would be the most effective way of securing peace and stability in the post war world. The ‹heart and the stomach and the liver of the organisation› would be the provision of a veto to the major global powers: Russia, Britain, America, China and France which would allow the largest countries to better manage the affairs of the smaller ones.

The language of human rights would provide a moral justification to this new world order, which would place stability and enduring peace as the highest priority of international relations. The idea that human rights laws could embody human dignity meant they could be made sacrosanct, and above the political concerns of the countries signing up to them. In other words, they could resist the influence of national populaces. But this utopian vision did not last long. Right from the beginning, disagreements about the provisions of the Universal Declaration illuminated the disparate and divergent political positions of the contributing counties. The attempt to craft an apolitical, democratically removed baseline for all the countries of the world, one situated in the primacy of human 'dignity' was immediately stalled by the social and political realities of the signatory states.

Again, the fear of bolstering socialism in Europe was at the forefront of concerns for both the UK and the US. They worked hard to squeeze out a 'right of political rebellion' from the early drafts of the Universal Declaration. Both countries had experienced widespread civil disobedience in the early parts of the 20th century, from an organised and increasingly militant working class. The idea of bolstering these movements with human rights protections was politically unpalatable. While the Deceleration included social and economic rights, the precise meanings of what these rights would entail was hotly disputed. The British defined social and economic rights narrowly, as providing for some sort of social insurance. Other countries, including Panama and Venezuela, conceived of social and economic rights as providing 'social security from the cradle to the grave'. It was simply not possible to create a document which could allay the fears of socialism from one part of the globe with the active promotion of socialist principles from another.

Accordingly, the Universal Deceleration was not a radical document. Rather 'it accurately reflected the conservative social mores and liberal economic values of the immediate post-war era'. Sellers notes that 'it proclaimed trade union rights and the rights to enter into and dissolve marriage freely but also reaffirmed the family as the natural and fundamental unit in society' and carefully reasserted the 'right to own property'. Much like the drafters of the European Convention on Human Rights, the drafters of the Declaration were driven by conservative principles and an overriding concern to ensure stability. Their concern to enshrine the right to private property reflected their concerns about the spread of socialism, a fear shared by the drafters of the European Convention. Today, it is the fear of democracy that echoes in our arguments about human rights. This fear is shared today by both the left and right.

Human rights in the UK

There were two important contexts to the passing of the human rights act and the incorporation of the European Convention into UK law. The first was the reorientation of the Labour party. The Act was introduced among a package of 'constitutional reforms' which also included devolution and the reform of the House of Lords. This focus on constitutional reform, which had historically been of interest only to a narrow group of Tory peers, arose in the early 1990s following two electoral defeats for Labour in the 1980s and the apparent discrediting of their traditional social democratic agenda. The passing of the Human Rights Act spoke to a Labour leadership who had reoriented itself around the cosmopolitan middle classes and away from their traditional working-class base.

Labour justified the focus on constitutional reform by arguing that there was a 'crisis in public confidence' in democratic institutions. What Labour meant by 'constitutional reform' was bolstering the role of the Judiciary in order to address this crisis. For New Labour, the Judiciary could fix a lack of public faith in the institutions of democracy. This was a historic reversal for Labour, who had been suspicious of the Judiciary, 'public school boys in wigs' as one prominent Labour MP of the 1970s described them, being passed too much control over the democratic process.

The second important context was the increasing politicisation of the Judiciary. Studies from the late 1990s explained how the role of the Judiciary had shifted since the 1970s, from interpreters of the law to makers of the law. An increasingly political role placed pressure on the Judiciary to become more diverse and more accountable to the public[17]. This trend was well underway by the time Labour announced plans to incorporate the European convention.

Their authoritarian tendencies in government meant that by 2006, the Human Rights Act had become a bugbear for the Labour party[18]. Tony Blair was considering radical reform of the Act by 2006, which would have allowed parliament to overrule the decisions of Judges on Human Rights issues[19]. But by that point The Human Rights Act had shown itself to be largely irrelevant in the context of Labour's attacks on civil liberties. It had done nothing to prevent the enormous expansion of the criminal law into new areas of people's lives. It had done nothing to protect the long-standing rights of defendants, which Labour had relentlessly attacked. At best, history had shown the Human Rights Act to be a political vanity project for the lawyerly classes, which did little or nothing to protect fundamental freedoms. At its worst, it had served its purpose as a convenient way for Labour to satisfy liberal voters of its liberal credentials while bulldozing many of the rights that the convention purported to defend.

Labour's embrace of Human Rights

The Labour party was born from working class agitation. In the 19th Century, British capitalism had rapidly expanded leading to a huge increase in the British industrial workforce. The franchise had also expanded, firstly in 1867 and then in 1884, to include significantly more working-class voters. Working class agitation had also manifested itself around the campaigns for increased suffrage. Towards the end of the 19th Century, this upsurge in political awareness among the working class resulted in the formation of the first trade unions and the establishment of the

Trades Union Congress in 1868.

In 1900, at London's Union Hall, a new organisation was formed called the Labour Representation Committee. It was constituted by a network of labour unions and a number of socialist societies with the explicit aim of representing the interests of working people in parliament. The LRC dramatically increased its affiliations in 1901 and 1903 following the Taff Vale decision that made trade unions liable for damages incurred by an employer during a strike. It was in 1906 that a loose political coalition of groups around the LRC adopted the name the Labour Party[20].

Over the course of the 20th century, the Labour Party became a means for reconciling the working class with the interests of bourgeoisie society. In the years before World War One, it channelled working class political agitation towards the reform of capitalism and against its overthrow. During the First World War, the Labour party was instrumental in ensuring the British working class supported the War effort. The then leader Arthur Henderson issued statements to quell the anger against conscription, to prevent the unions from striking and to prevent any disruption to the war time economy through working class agitation[21].

Representing the interests of the working class within the constraints of capitalism meant that the Labour party were often forced to subjugate the needs of the workers to the interests of capitalism. In 1929 unemployment was at a record level of 2.5 million. The Labour government announced in 1931 that it was cutting public spending by £97 million, two thirds of which was to come from a 20 percent cut in employment benefit. National insurance contributions would also be increased. It is worth remembering that while Jeremy Corbyn's Labour party opposes Tory cuts to public services, his party has a long history of anti-working class responses to moments of economic crisis.

Between 1951 and 1959, the party lost three general elections and the support of 1.7 million voters. A period of economic boom made the left wing of the Labour party appear increasingly irrelevant. A new tendency within the party gained popularity who unequivocally rejected the need for class struggle, instead arguing to 'eradicate class and create in its place a sense of common interest and equal status'. By 1959, senior Labour leaders were arguing for the weakening of connections with the Trade Union movement, citing the growth of white collar workers, the decline in working class identity and the growth of consumerism. It was Gaskill, the leader of the Labour party in 1959, who first proposed the repeal of its clause 4 – which committed the party to bringing about socialism – a move which would later be enacted by Tony Blair.

In 1983, the Labour party published its election manifesto which would become known as the 'longest suicide note in history' under their then leader Michael Foot. Michael Foot would be thought of by many as the last socialist leader of the Labour party. The manifesto embodied many of the demands associated with the Left wing of the Labour party including nationalisation of key public services and unilateral nuclear disarmament. The document even mentioned human rights, claiming that they objected to 'human rights violations wherever they occurred' and whatever the political makeup of the government found to be violating them. In the lead up to the 1983 general election, Labour saw defeats in long standing Labour seats including Bermondsey in South London. In the general election that followed Labour was reduced to 209 seats to a Conservative total of 397 seats.

It was widely perceived at the time that the 1983 election result saw the left of the party once again discredited. One commentator on the night said, echoing many of the remarks made about the party today, that there was no 'credible opposition government in waiting because the Labour party has drifted far too far to the Left'.

Neil Kinnock was elected party leader shortly after the 1983 electoral defeat. Kinnock was widely touted as a reformer and deeply hostile to the radical left of the party. He surrounded himself with a new generation of advisors to assist him in drawing the party back towards the centre. These included Peter Mandelson who had been chairman of the British Youth Council and who would become known as Labour's first 'spin doctor'. A young Jack Straw also came to work for Kinnock, having been elected to his parliamentary seat in Blackburn in 1979. This influx of new ministers would be followed in 1983 with the election to parliament of a young Tony Blair and Gordon Brown.

By the middle of the 1980s, the centre of the Labour party was in all out conflict with the far left. In a now famous speech to the 1985 Labour party conference, in what came to be known as 'that speech', Neil Kinnock famously condemned the 'outdated... misplaced dogma' of left factions within the Labour party.

Labour under Neil Kinnock unexpectedly lost a second general election in 1992. The failure to win the 1992 general election led to the replacement of Neil Kinnock with John Smith. Smith was a Scottish lawyer who had served as Solicitor general in Scotland and was a long standing law officer. Smith was largely seen to be continuing the process of reform started by Kinnock. Smith was responsible for promoting those who would become key personnel in the first Labour government, many of whom were drawn from the legal profession. Tony Blair (a barrister) became Home Secretary, where he rapidly sought to rebrand the Labour party as the 'party of law and order'. Jack Straw (another barrister) became shadow minister for local government and housing. Lord Derry Irvine (senior barrister) was made shadow Lord Chancellor.

Labour and Tories on freedom

Before coming to power, Labour went through a policy convergence with the Tory party over political freedom. This was illustrated in the passage of two key pieces of legislation. The Public Order Act of 1994 sparked wide spread opposition among the general public for its absurd powers with respect to preventing 'raves'. Under section 63 of that Act, the police were given the power to 'direct' persons suspected of preparing a rave to leave a particular area of land. The Act was made famous by its absurd characterisation of a 'music' as 'including sounds wholly or predominantly characterised by the emission of a succession of repetitive beats'. Perhaps even worse was Section 65, allowing any uniformed constable who believed a person is on their way to a rave within a five-mile radius to stop them and direct them away from the area; non-compliant citizens may be subject to a maximum fine not exceeding £1000.

The Public Order Act also significantly modified a defendant's right to silence. In 1972 the Criminal Law Revision Committee had recommended that Courts should be allowed to draw 'such inferences...as appear proper' from the failure of an accused to mention to the police any fact which was later relied on in his defence. In 1987, the then Home Secretary Douglas Hurd gave a speech to the Police Foundation in which he asked 'does the current law really protect the innocent whose interests will generally lie in answering police questions frankly?' In other words: if you have nothing to fear, you have nothing to hide.

In July 1989 a working group report was published that further recommended a significant dilution of the right to silence. It claimed that the right favoured 'professional crooks' and that innocent people had nothing to fear from answering questions. The recommendations of the report were targeted at what the report called the 'ambush defence'. The central recommendation of that report was the introduction of a caution that would warn suspects that any failure to mention a fact which they later relied on in their defence could be held against them in Court.

This slow attack on a fundamental principle of the justice system, the right to silence, was ushered in with little political opposition. Labour opposition to the Public Order bill was minimal. One commentator observed that 'presumably for fear of being seen to be soft on crime...the Labour party declined to oppose the bill on Second Reading' and as a result 'serious opposition was negligible'. A young Tony Blair moved an amendment to the legislation which required the right to silence provisions to only apply once a defendant was present in a police station and not before he had received legal advice from a lawyer. The amendment was defeated. It fell to the liberal democrats to provide what opposition there was to the bill, but they could not prevent its passage into law.

The second key piece of legislation that showed a policy convergence around civil liberties was the Police Act of 1997. The Act was one of the final pieces of legislation of the Conservative administration and 'reemphasised the conservative commitment to strong law-and-order policies' before the 1997 general election. This law introduced a regime for the disclosure of criminal records as part of the employment process. Today, the checking of criminal records has become the norm. But at the time, this law represented a significant expansion of the state's power to hold and disclose personal information. The Act established the Criminal Records Agency which was the first national database of criminal records. The Act allowed for 'enhanced' criminal records checks, which would reveal arrests and cautions as well as criminal convictions. Again, the law was rushed through with minimal opposition.

Labour did not pose any significant opposition to these significant incursions on civil liberties. In fact, it was in the years before and after this bill that the Labour government began echoing the sentiments of the law, the idea that the rights of criminal defendants were just inconveniences to be overcome, in an attempt to portray Labour as the real party of 'law and order'. Labour's acquiescence to new draconian laws foreshadowed their commitment to being 'tough on crime and tough on the causes of crime'. The Human Rights Act, which passed greater control over civil liberties to the Judiciary, was not the 'one liberal thing' done by the New Labour government. It was a logical extension of its aversion to civil liberty, which had already been illustrated during its period in opposition.

Incorporating The European Convention – a Lawyer's pet project

Incorporating the European Convention into UK law was not a response to public pressure. It was largely a political cause of a small number of specialised lawyers and campaign groups. The barrister and author Marcel Berlins described how appeals to incorporate the Act fell largely on deaf ears between the 1960s and its incorporation in 2000. Lawyers with sufficient specialism could already take cases to the European Court and had done so, but even among specialists there was a recognition that the European Court of Human Rights was run by Judges who tended to be 'less sophisticated' than their British Judicial colleagues. Given that the convention was already having an impact on UK Courts, the case for actually incorporating it into UK law was not widely considered. In fact, there were some who recognised that the European model of freedom could be narrower than that protected under the English common law. One paper in 1976 said of the convention that while 'it is true that Britain, now a member of the EEC, is now bound by the European Convention on Human Rights it (gives) a very general definition of human rights which may not fit easily into the more precise nature of English law'.

Attempts at codifying British Rights had always been a concern of Tories. There were a number of attempts between 1970 and 1990 to introduce a British Bill of Rights into UK Law, which would codify civil liberties protections in statute. These did not receive popular support. Viewed cynically, it is not surprising that many of the people lobbying for such a bill were lawyers.

The purpose of a bill of rights would be to introduce a way that people could sue based on violations of their liberties. The only difference that introducing a codified bill of rights would achieve would be the ability to 'enforce' these rights through the Courts. This would inevitably mean litigation. Incorporating British rights into a single Bill had the potential to open up a whole new practice area for well-heeled lawyers. Few outside of the legal establishment saw the point.

The incorporation of the European Convention only presented itself as a serious possibility when Labour began to focus on constitutional reform. Constitutional reform had become a significant focus for Labour policy in the aftermath of their electoral defeats in the 1983 and 1987 general elections. The rigorous policy revision which followed these two defeats culminated in the first major policy document to focus on constitutional reform: *Meet the Challenge Make the Change*. The policy paper influenced the 1992 election manifesto, which put constitutional reform at the forefront of Labour electoral policy for the first time.

Constitutional reform had only been of real interest to Tory Lords. It was a Tory peer Lord Hailsham who had argued the need for democratic reform when during a Halsbury Lecture he coined the phrase 'elected dictatorship' to describe the excessive power of the UK executive[22]. Hailsham argued that the UK constitution allowed the government too much power to act without the authority of parliament.

Lord Derry Irvine was made John Smith's Shadow Lord Chancellor and was Blair's first Lord Chancellor when Labour won power. Irvine was responsible for developing Labour's programme of constitutional reform. Irvine had been a successful commercial barrister before becoming Tony Blair's first Lord Chancellor after they took power in 1997. His chambers had a particular commercial focus on public law, of which human rights would form a part. Irvine was a long-time confidant of the

Blairs and had been Cherie and Tony's pupil master while they were pupil barristers. When Irvine was eventually sacked from his role after Labour won a second term, it was widely portrayed as a betrayal of a close personal friendship.

Labour's constitutional reform was targeted at remedying a perceived crisis of confidence in political institutions. In a speech in 1998, Irvine described how Labour's constitutional reform was focused on 'wide ranging modernisation', citing a 'national crisis of confidence in the political system'[23]. Irvine went on to describe a 'lack of clarity about individual rights and how they should be enforced', notwithstanding 'half a century of experience' under the European Convention. By including the Human Rights Act in a programme of reform that targeted a 'crisis of confidence' in British political institutions, Irvine indicated that he saw the law as capable of remedying that crisis. He was anticipating increased judicial involvement in political decision making.

The discussion that arose following the policy announcements around the Act was targeted at the legally educated. Jack Straw commented on the publication of the paper that proceeded the Human Rights Bill 'Bringing Rights Home' that anyone who thought these were 'foreign laws...clearly had not read the provisions of the European Convention' and did not properly understand the nature of legal rights in the UK. Of course, these aloof and pompous defences of the Act presupposed a knowledge of how the Courts worked in the first place According to parliamentary reports, the debates around the bill were so technical that those MPs with legal training dominated. The discussion around the legislation was clearly geared towards those who already understood the relationship between the English Courts and Strasbourg which was a very small portion of the population.

The move to incorporate the European Convention into UK law did not come about as a result of any popular pressure. It arose because a small group of lawyers at the head of the Labour party fitted it awkwardly into a package of 'constitutional reforms' which they thought could remedy a 'crisis of confidence' in UK institutions. While these reforms were purportedly designed to make the UK 'more democratic' the incorporation of the Convention through the 1998 Act merely increased the role of the judiciary in deciding the extent of our political freedom. At the same time, New Labour began a crackdown on civil liberties that would last throughout their period in government.

Bonfire of the Liberties

The passage of the Act did not instil a new respect for Civil Liberty in the organs of government. In fact, it has become trite to point out New Labour's dreadful record on civil liberties while in power. During Labour's period in office it is estimated that a staggering 4,300 new criminal offences were created and over fifty new criminal justice public order and related bills were introduced. The prison population increased 35 percent between 1997 and 2008. New Labour also bulldozed a number of rights traditionally afforded to defendants in the criminal justice system. They continued an attack on the right to silence that had been started by Major's government, ended double jeopardy, allowed for the introduction of previously inadmissible character evidence. They also introduced the most draconian anti-terror regime in recent British history.

New Labour expanded police powers of stop and search and introduced further powers to impose punishments on people without having to criminally prosecute them. They significantly expanded the state's surveillance powers through the Regulation of Investigatory Powers Act. This Act gave powers to a wide range of public bodies to undertake intrusive surveillance. The introduction of Anti-Social Behaviour Orders has been described as an example of increasing measures of 'restriction without conviction', because they allowed for significant restrictions on liberty without having to rely on a criminal conviction. The use of ASBOs exploded under New Labour having been introduced by the Crime and Disorder Act of 1998.

An audit by the Convention on Modern Liberty in 2009 set out the full extent of powers introduced by New Labour. Henry Porter of the convention on modern liberty said that New Labour 'swept away many centuries-old rights...We now have that evidence [and can] oppose what is happening to one of the world's oldest democracies.". Only that opposition never truly materialised. We will see in the chapters to come that a brief period of rebellion against the New Labour legislative programme would not survive the terror attacks against the UK.

The years immediately after the passage of the Human Rights Act have been described as a 'bonfire of the liberties'. The passage of legislation immediately after the Human Rights Act showed how the European human rights model was completely ineffective at safeguarding freedom. What recent years have shown us is that a Judiciary that is more focused on rights based jurisprudence is not necessarily conducive to a political culture that respects civil liberties.

Conclusion

The ascendency of human rights in the aftermath of the Second World War was part of an attempt by the European elite to manage the influence of democracy. The primary threat they were seeking to defend themselves from was the spread of socialism. The architects of the human rights regime were attempting to re-establish the position of European Christian values, which they perceived to be threatened by democratic changes. Internationally, the human rights framework provided a powerful moral justification for transnational institutions like the UN and European Union.

The adoption of Human Rights by the Labour party was part of a scattergun process of 'constitutional reform', which sought to pass greater power over to the Judiciary, a step that the left wing of the party had always been deeply sceptical of. The passing of the Act foreshadowed significant assaults on civil liberty and defendants' rights which left people less able to defend themselves against state power. Today, the left imagine that human rights laws are a guarantor for freedom. They have bought into the founding myth of the human rights project: that judges are better guardians of freedom than the people.

Today, the first step towards developing a freer society would be to debunk this myth. Human rights have done little to protect our freedom. They have instead presided over their collapse. In the next chapter we will consider recent events and official responses. We will see that the way we understand the ability of the law to regulate risk is likely to be central to our debate around freedom in the years to come.

Terror and freedom: Four attacks

Attacks on civil liberties are not new. A brief survey of scholarly work on the legal history of the 20th century reveals a grim picture[24]. In almost every decade, historians can cite appalling violations of civil liberties against particular groups. In the 1930s British communists were routinely denied due process and their right to freedom of expression in the course of the government's crackdown on their activities. In the 1970s, those accused of involvement in Irish nationalist politics could be detained without charge, interviewed without a lawyer and tried without a jury. That was before the brutal conditions that faced many Irish nationalists if they were locked up. Homosexuals were legally persecuted through the criminal law arguably until the 1990s. Every generation can point to those who have had their freedom ignored by legal institutions. While political freedom is considered the backbone of the English constitution, it is striking that we have arguably never had a distinctively pro-civil liberties government.

This is why any argument that human rights laws 'protect the human', as claimed in Amnesty International's tagline, are ludicrous. As we will see in the cases to come, democratic pressure has been a far more reliable safeguard for individual freedom than human rights laws. Irish Catholics did not receive any help from the European Court of Human Rights in their struggles for freedom. They were told that the subjugation of their liberty was part of an entirely legitimate 'derogation' by the Irish state. They had to resort to political action to defend themselves. British gays could not make a human rights complaint to correct the inherently homophobic laws that were used to persecute them for decades. They had to campaign, on the streets, for legal reform which eventually came. Terror suspects today experience roughly similar treatment to those who the state despised in the past. This is why it is absurd that today, resistance to anti-freedom measures take the form of human rights complaints. Political problems have been reduced to the level of individual rights violations. We have reduced politics to law.

This is why a growth in respect for human rights can coincide with a decline in respect for civil liberties. As we have taken our place among a 'hegemony' of human rights, we are in fact becoming less and less free. This chapter will explore the position of civil liberties in contemporary society, particularly in the context of recent terror attacks in the UK.

Freedom is 'back in fashion'

The Conservative party and the Liberal Democrats governed Britain after a hung parliament following the 2010 general election. The hung parliament resulted in a coalition government between the Liberal Democrats, led by Nick Clegg, and the Conservative party, led by David Cameron. It is often forgotten that in the early days of this coalition government, civil liberties provided a common cause between these two politically disparate parties.

The conservative manifesto in 2010 featured an implicit recognition that Civil Liberties had suffered significant defeats under New Labour. It promised to 'restore our civil liberties' and noted how 'Labour have subjected Britain's historic freedoms to unprecedented attack. They have trampled on liberties and, in their place, compiled huge databases to track the activities of millions of perfectly innocent people, giving public bodies extraordinary powers to intervene in the way we live our lives'. The conservative manifesto was built on a promise to reverse the trend towards eroding civil liberties that had emerged under New Labour[25].

A purported commitment to civil liberties gave ground for agreement between the two coalition parties in the aftermath of the election. During the campaign, both parties had expressed interest in repealing New Labour's 'database state'. The Lib Dems had drafted a freedom bill in February 2009, the first draft of which included a pledge to ensure a right to trial by jury for all offences and scrapping the contact point database. The Lib Dem website proclaimed:

'This is not intended to be an exhaustive list of all the freedoms that have been lost in recent years. Sadly, there are too many. It is intended to be a starting point – to show people how much personal liberty has been stripped away by this Government and the one before it'.

David Cameron had said that a Great Repeal Bill would be the foundation for the next queen's speech were he to win power. The proposed bill would scrap ID cards and repeal large sections of the new criminal law introduced by New Labour criminal justice legislation. This latter promise was crucial. It was in the voluminous criminal justice legislation introduced by New Labour that many of the most significant inroads into free speech and freedom of association had been made. Following the election, the coalition agreement said it believed the British state had become 'too authoritarian' and promised to 'implement a full programme of measures to reverse the substantial erosion of civil liberties and roll back state intrusion'. The two parties had, according to their agreement, been 'bound together' by a common interest in restoring civil liberties that had been lost under Labour.

The rhetoric around civil liberties continued into 2011. In his 'Restoring British Liberties' speech in January 2011, the Deputy Prime Minister, Nick Clegg, said: 'Our Labour predecessors will be remembered as the Government who took your freedoms away. We want to be remembered as the ones who gave them back.' The deputy prime minister later remarked that 'freedom was back in fashion'[26]. Reaching out to the Liberal Democrats, David Cameron said in his speech following the 2010 election results: 'We share a common commitment to civil liberties and to getting rid immediately of Labour's ID card scheme'[27].

Commentators in the UK reacted to this apparent new consensus around civil liberties positively. One writer remarked how the coalition consensus around civil liberties could give rise to a 'golden age' for freedom. "Any moves to reverse the tide of authoritarian legislation we've seen over the last few years are warmly welcome," said Daniel Hamilton in 2011, campaign director for the civil liberties campaign group Big Brother Watch. It appeared to those concerned with preserving freedom that the coalition government represented an opportunity to reverse the excesses of the New Labour government.

The Labour opposition, led by Ed Miliband, even accused the new coalition of placing civil liberties rhetoric above the need to keep the public safe. Labour MP Yvette Cooper, then Shadow Home Secretary, said following the announcement of the coalition's Freedom Bill that the government was at risk of putting 'political rhetoric' (about freedom and civil liberty) above the evidence from experts with regard to combatting terror. 'They are going too far on DNA retention and are going against the evidence that shows it has a significant impact bringing serious criminals to justice and exonerating innocent people'.

Yet this climate of appreciation was short lived. What we learned in the years that followed 2010, first with the coalition government and then subsequently under a Tory majority, is that events have significant power in the contemporary climate to shape official attitudes to political freedom. It is the spasmodic, often unthinking reaction to tragedy which shapes our contemporary discussion around freedom. This speaks to an overwhelming ambivalence on behalf of our governments to civil liberties and a complete disorientation in the face of political violence.

Woolwich

The first sign that civil liberties would not fare as well as expected under the coalition government was the Communications

Data Bill, which would become popularly known as the 'Snoopers Charter'. In 2012, a draft Communications Data Bill was introduced to parliament. It introduced new and incredibly broad powers for the state to require data retention and provision by service providers. The law would effectively allow the state to require communications companies to store huge amounts of data about our communications and to make them available for the authorities for the purpose of investigating crime.

In 2012, a joint committee of Lords and MPs rubbished the Snooper's Charter saying the wording of the bill was too broad and arcane. The bill would allow for 'fishing expeditions' on the part of the intelligence agencies, rather than targeted surveillance. In April 2013, Nick Clegg announced that the bill would not proceed while the Liberal Democrats were in government. His announcement was largely credited with keeping the bill out of the 2013 Queen's Speech.

The fortunes of the bill changed dramatically when, in May 2013, fusilier Lee Rigby was murdered on the streets of Woolwich in South London. Michael Adebolajo and Michael Adebowale drove a car into the 25 year old fusilier as he was returning to his barracks from the nearby train station. They then stabbed repeatedly at his neck in an attempt to decapitate him. Adebolajo then gave an incoherent and rambling speech about British foreign policy to an assembled crowd, some of whom had caught the aftermath of the incident on their mobile phones. The incident was reported as London's first terrorist attack since the July 7th bombings.

Woolwich is commonly remembered as the first act of terrorism which focused on the mass distribution of imagery. Adebolajo's speech in the middle of the road, in the immediate aftermath of the murder, was a piece of performance designed to be widely distributed online. It has since been called the first piece of 'viral terrorism', an act which focused more on the potential impact of images of the incident over and above the impact of the incident itself[28].

The government responded in kind. The then Home Secretary Theresa May convened a meeting of the Cobra committee, to formulate what she termed a 'national response'. Adebolajo's face appeared across national newspapers the following day under headlines that read 'the face of terror'. The incident quickly became referred to as the 'Woolwich terror attack'.

In this aftermath of the attack, the Liberal Democrats came under criticism for their opposition to the Communications bill. Only hours after Rigby had been killed, two Labour peers Lord West and Lord Reid, claimed that the attacks showed that opposition to the bill was 'putting the country at risk'[29]. Criticism also came from within the party. Liberal Democrat peer Lord Carlisle repeated his calls for the bill to be introduced, telling BBC's news night programme that 'we must ensure that the police and the security services have for the future the tools they need that will enable them to prevent this kind of attack taking place'[30].

The question that was not asked at the time of the attack was whether any increased intelligence powers would have made any difference. Both Michael Adebolajo and Michael Adebowale were known to the security services. The Regulation of Investigatory Powers Act (RIPA) already granted powers to intercept communications of those who were 'on the radar'. The men were not working as part of any broader organisation. Further individuals were arrested in the aftermath of the murder for involvement in a conspiracy to kill Rigby, but no charges were brought. No one has been able, in the 4 years since the attack, to provide any piece of information or evidence that would have been available had the communications bill been law at the time of the attack. It was not at all clear that any new surveillance powers would have made any difference at all.

Yet the call to 'do something' in response to Woolwich was powerful. Almost immediately after the Woolwich attack, the

Liberal Democrats began to retreat from their defiance over the IP bill. In an interview with LBC a week after the attack Nick Clegg said that the government would be 'pursuing some parts' of the IP bill. Clegg said he would not support the elements of the bill which would store information about the websites being visited by users but would support efforts to link IP addresses to specific devices. He said 'the British public want us politicians to strike a very difficult balance of freedom, democracy and traditions of liberty and giving security services and police the tools they need."

Woolwich demonstrated how official understanding of events can rapidly change the fortunes of draconian laws. Had the incident been understood in the same terms as the many other knife crime incidents that occur in the capital every year, albeit a particular distressing one, calls to legislate would have lacked credibility. As terror lawyer David Anderson QC said in the aftermath of the attack, the designation of a particular offence as 'terrorist' had the power to make further calls for legislation appear more forceful. He said '"Terrorism law gives excessive weight to the idea that terrorism is different, losing sight of the principle that terrorism is above all crime, and that special laws to deal with it need to be justified by the peculiar nature of the crime". The need to 'do something' in the face of terror had overridden the need to think about what good that something might do.

Prevent and phantom powers

However, the move towards more draconian laws has been qualified by an alarming lack of deployment. As well as introducing draconian new surveillance laws, the coalition and subsequent Tory majority government have been responsible for introducing a number of laws that are not widely deployed. They have also invested large sums in developing a Prevent agenda, which does little to combat terrorism but which has been blamed for sewing division among minority communities and limiting free speech.

On the 12th of February 2015, the Counter Terrorism and Security Act received royal assent. The Act purported to 'combat the underlying ideology that feeds supports and sanctions terrorism'. Section one of the Act gave the authorities, via schedule 1, the power of seizure and temporary retention of travel documents where a person is suspected of intending to leave Great Britain or the United Kingdom in connection with terrorism-related activity. This power was targeted at those leaving the UK to fight for the Islamic State.

Section 2 of the Act introduced the controversial Temporary Exclusion Orders (TEOs). These allowed for a mechanism to intervene where suspected terrorists were returning from abroad. It gave the Secretary of State the power to refuse entry to the UK where certain conditions were met, which included where they reasonably suspect that the individual had been involved in 'terrorism related activity' outside the UK.

Understanding how broad this power is requires understanding some other aspects of UK terror legislation. Terror activity is largely defined by reference to the 'proscribed organisations' under the Terrorism Act. This list indicates which organisations the UK government consider to be terrorist. Once an organisation becomes designated it is extremely difficult to be removed. This is why the Act still 'proscribes' a number of completely redundant Irish republican organisations.

In 2011, the New Labour system of control orders was repealed and replaced with Terrorism Prevention and Investigation Measures (TPIMs). In 2016 we learned that no more than 10 people had ever been subject to TPIMs. In 2014, it was revealed that only 1 person had been made subject to a TPIM in the course of that year. TPIMs allowed for highly draconian controls to be placed over the lives of terror suspects, including effectively placing them under house arrest and significantly reducing their access to communication technology. The upper Courts set out case law in 2014 saying that the use of the orders had to be restricted to truly exceptional cases. This has resulted in a scenario where barely any orders are made at all.

This further exposes the lack of serious thinking about how to respond to terror. Introducing broad powers is shown to be woefully inadequate when those powers are not deployed. These powers do not reveal an authoritarian state. They show a worrying lack of engagement with the reality of policing terror.

This disengagement from reality is illustrated further in the absurd Prevent programme. In the six years after the 2005 London bombings, £80 million was spent on 1,000 prevent schemes across 94 different local authorities. The New Labour government ran its Prevent programme under the heading of 'community cohesion', suggesting that anti-terror measures were being used to promote a particular set of values rather than targeting specific threats.

The Prevent strategy has notoriously suffered from a lack of clear parameters. The Counter Terror and Security Act 2015 created a general duty on public bodies to prevent people being drawn into terrorism. This meant that Universities, hospitals and other public institutions became stand-ins for terror police and fell under an obligation to report people they considered to be at risk. With respect to schools, OFSTED could monitor whether a school was abiding by its statutory duty and schools could be marked badly for failing to properly engage. With such vague parameters, and such harsh punishments for falling short, it is hardly surprising that the Act has been misapplied. One student, a Mohammed Umar Farooq, was interviewed in September 2015 by Staffordshire University under the auspices of Prevent after being seen to be reading a text book on terrorism. He was studying for a Master's Degree in terrorist studies.

The Prevent strategy has led to a number of other serious embarrassments for the UK government. In 2014 it was revealed that 200 CCTV cameras in the Muslim areas of Birmingham, 72 of which had been hidden, were partly funded by money from the Home Office's counter terrorism operations. The areas of Birmingham that had been targeted with cameras were known to be majority Muslim areas. The scheme was known as 'project Champion'. An investigation by the Guardian newspaper revealed that the police had misled local residents into believing that the cameras were to be used to combat vehicle crime and anti-social behaviour. The cameras were in fact paid for from a grant from a government fund called the 'Terrorism and Allied matters' fund. These moments of embarrassment underscored the sinister nature of Prevent, which encouraged a culture of suspicion and distrust around particular communities. These measures were all the more wrongheaded, given that the attackers that have struck the UK rarely emanate from any established religious community.

Prevent has also had a significant impact on higher education. Academics complain of being turned into spies for the intelligence agencies as they are forced to consider every one of their students as a potential radical. In 2017, it was revealed that Kings College London, one of the country's leading Universities, had warned its staff and its students that their emails may be retained en masse in order to comply with their duty under Prevent. Not only is this poisonous for the relationship between students and their teachers, but is also places significant strain on academic freedom.

Prevent is a nasty and counterproductive scheme. It encourages suspicion and erodes trust between people. It also does not work. As we will see, real life terrorists have been completely missed by Prevent even though they 'fit the profile' of a terrorist perfectly. Those who do undertake terrorist attacks rarely appear to have undergone any kind of 'radicalisation' on University campuses or at the hands of public bodies. Instead, terrorists who attack European countries have overwhelmingly been withdrawn social misfits who rarely engage in the world around them. With a few exceptions, Prevent could not possibly have picked up on these lonely young men. Where it could have done, as in the case of Salman Abedi discussed below, it failed to do so.

Westminster

In March 2017, Khalid Masood drove his car into 10 people on Westminster Bridge before crashing into the gates of Westminster Palace. He then stabbed a policeman in the neck before being shot. The attack happened round the corner from where I work in St Pauls.

Whereas the response to Woolwich was characterised by a level of panic and hyperbole, the response to Westminster was arguably more measured. Theresa May spoke the following morning of the 'spirit of freedom' that ran through the streets of Westminster. People called the speech 'defiant'. Guardian columnist Simon Jenkins captured a prevailing public view that Masood's actions should be seen as a 'crime' rather than a terrorist attack. ISIS claimed responsibility for the attack, but this quickly became understood to be an opportunistic way of garnering publicity. A number of leading commentators seriously put the case that we should resist the temptation to discuss the attack in terms of terrorism at all.

It became clear within a week of the attack that Masood had no connections to international terrorism. The Metropolitan police said that while he 'clearly had an interest in Jihad' there was 'no evidence of any connection between Masood and either the Islamic State or Al Qaeda'. He had been born in Dartford, Kent and given the name Adrian Elms. He had grown up in the seaside town of Rye in East Sussex, later moving to Tunbridge Wells in Kent. He had been a keen footballer. Immediately prior to the attack he had been based in the West Midlands and had accumulated a string of convictions for violent crime.

Whereas with respect to Woolwich, the authorities had been vociferous about the connection with terrorism, with respect to Masood every effort was made to present him as nihilistic and lacking any ideological motivation.

Notwithstanding the measured public response to the attack, politicians still targeted civil liberties in the aftermath of Westminster. The focus of government attention was on terrorist propaganda and communication technology. Two days after the attack, a spokesperson for number 10 said that social-media companies 'have a responsibility when it comes to making sure [extremist] material is not disseminated... we are always talking with them on how they are to achieve that'. Then, rather menacingly, he said 'the ball is in their court'. In short: take action or we will.

The Home Secretary Amber Rudd then appeared on the Andrew Marr programme on the Sunday after the attack, saying that the police were unable to access Masood's WattsApp internet messaging facility due to encryptions. She claimed that the police were unable to read key messages sent by Masood using the online messaging service because of the company's end to end encryption. Rudd even went on to say that WattsApp had provided a 'secret space' for terrorists to communicate with impunity. The Daily Mail newspaper was mocked for posting an article labelling websites including YouTube, WhatsApp and Twitter as terrorist 'safe havens'.

The government's calls for greater internet regulation appeared completely out of nowhere. There had never been any suggestion that the Westminster attack could have been prevented if the security services had further powers. In fact, many pointed out that the police can already access WattsApp messaging from a person's handset. The announcement seemed intuitive on behalf of the government, as though the very fact of the attack called for some kind of corrective action in law.

The reaction to Westminster shows how unthinking government

responses to terror can be. In the aftermath of 9/11, it became common to think of growing governmental surveillance as a developing 'big brother' state. Allusions to 1984 were common in describing the attempts of governments to monitor more of our behaviour. Yet, in the aftermath of these attacks in the UK, the overwhelming feeling was that our state was confused about how to respond. George Orwell's Big Brother represented an organised system of state intrusion. Today's government seems completely confused by comparison.

Later in 2017, a further attack on Manchester was met by mounting fears around Islamophobia. Manchester was arguably the most vicious attack in our history. Yet in the months following the attack, the sense of inaction was palpable. In the aftermath of Manchester the profound failure of government to cope with the threat of Islamist violence was exposed, along with a dangerous reluctance to address its real nature.

Manchester

The attack on an Ariana Grande concert in Manchester, which killed 22 people and injured over 100, was unique for its barbarity. The attacker Salman Abedi purposely targeted children who he thought were being oversexualised by Grande's music. He detonated a bomb in his rucksack in the foyer of the concert arena. Among those killed were many children and their parents. It was explicitly an attack not just on human beings, but on freedom itself.

Despite such an egregious attack, one which struck at the heart of Western values, the government's response to the attack was muted. There were no calls to introduce further security at concert venues. There were no calls for any further powers. This itself was bizarre, considering Abedi was part of a network and a known agitator against the British government.

Manchester demonstrated an oddly schizophrenic reaction on behalf of our authorities to the threat of terror. Whereas

Woolwich, a primitive attack killing one person, was deemed sufficient to give new energy to an entire surveillance framework, the drive to 'do something' seemed mooted in the aftermath of Manchester.

This reaction could perhaps be explained by the fact that more could have been done by the authorities to prevent the attack. Classmates of Abedi said that he 'fit the profile' of a suicide bomber, given that he had a short temper and was open to manipulation. When he was 16 he had fought against the Gaddafi regime in Libya. Reports to the BBC claimed that Abedi's father was a supporter of the radical cleric Abu Qatada, who he had met in London. He had been reported to terror hotlines twice for reportedly saying it was 'ok to suicide bomb'. If anyone should have been picked up by Prevent, or by our anti-terror framework, it ought to have been Abedi.

Yet in the aftermath of the attack, anger at what had occurred was discouraged. The idea that Manchester should be a cause to 'come together' was commonly expressed in the aftermath of the attack. Concerns about the possible rise in Islamophobic hate crime were often expressed. Greater Manchester police published statistics that suggested Islamophobic attacks had 'soared' by 505%. 'Hope, sadness and Islamophobia spreads' read one headline. The shock at the barbarity of the attack quickly gave way to concerns regarding the risk of Islamophobia.

The debate around Islamophobia in the aftermath of Manchester represented a significant diversion. Criminologists have noted how it is common for hate crime to spike in the aftermath of particular incidents. This is not necessarily evidence of hateful sentiment becoming more widespread. Instead, it is evidence that certain people who already hold certain viewpoints become emboldened to act on them for short periods immediately after a given attack. We have consistently seen such 'spikes' in reported hate crimes decrease rapidly in the months that follow. While it is right to express concern and investigate hate crime where it occurs, the focus on purported increases in Islamophobia over and above concerns about a terrorist attack further demonstrated disorientation and equivocation about how to respond.

The apparent failure to act in the face of Islamic terror is increasingly becoming a source of popular concern. In October 2017, a march took place in Central London. It was called the 'Football Lads Alliance' and described its aims as inviting the government to do something over Islamic terror. One of the participants explained to an interviewer that the march was inspired by the sense the government were 'doing nothing' to stop Islamic terror. The march gave voice to a particular narrative that emerged in the aftermath of the terror attacks: that the government would rather we mourn than get angry about what had taken place.

Today's climate has shifted markedly since the authoritarianism of New Labour post 9/11. Much of the framework that was used to discuss issues around political freedom seem redundant now. The trade-off between freedom and security does not accurately describe a society where increased law-making has not resulted in a greater feeling of security. 'Authoritarianism' does not accurately describe a state that seems disorientated by the threat of terror. This does not mean our state is impotent. In fact, the authorities have more power over our political freedoms than ever before. But their lack of authoritative response to terror means there is an understandable call to 'do more' in the face of appalling Islamist violence.

This makes freedom highly precarious in the modern age. The threats are three fold. Firstly, a government who resort to unthinking limitations on civil liberties in response to terror. Often, these responses are in the absence of any consideration about how a particular new power or law could make a difference to public safety. Secondly, a public who have been left with the impression that nothing has been done about the terror attacks threatening the UK. Third, a wider cultural disregard of the importance of fundamental freedoms. With no one in the public willing to stand up for free speech, freedom of assembly and freedom of religion on principle, they remain a consistent hostage to pragmatism. Human rights laws can do nothing to rejuvenate this principled respect for certain freedoms, because they encourage a qualified and judicially sanctioned version of how such freedoms should be conceived.

Human rights, moral cowardice

The European Court of Human Rights has not shied away from describing its purpose in moral terms. While judgements of the European Court reiterate that there is 'no uniform European conception of morals' and that each state retains a 'margin of appreciation' to determine their response to particular cases, they have also said that its approach to decision making is founded upon an 'adjudication of the moral dimension of human rights complaints in a way that is beneficial to the community of European states'. Dissenting judgements of the Court have complained of a 'lavish disregard of contemporary standards of morality' when accusing the Court of being too deferential to national Courts. This moralised role has been expressed by Judges on the Court and has raised doubts about impartiality. In 2006, a Turkish judge of the Court said 'I see my role not merely as a judge deciding cases but also as an intermediary between the Court's standards and the aspirations of Turkey to join the European Union'. This remark revealed the extent to which the European judiciary conceive of themselves as setting moral standards for national legislatures on behalf of the European Union.

While the Court has not been shy of attempting to shape a 'European morality' often, the answers they produce do not engage with the moral issue at the heart of a particular situation. Human rights judges do not decide whether it is right or wrong to treat an asylum seeker in a particular way or whether the right to die should be introduced into a particular country. Instead, they decide whether state action can be lawfully tolerated under the terms of the European Convention. In each case, they will assess the procedural steps taken by a state and assess whether enough was done to comply with the human rights laws.

However, human rights rhetoric is not just a legal phenomenon. Human rights supporters rely on human rights rhetoric in order to reduce the moral complexity of particular situations. The term 'human rights violations' is now used to describe behaviour in complex conflicts which is thought to be beyond the pale in some way. It is as though all is fair in love and war, except the violation of human rights.

This creates a deeply distorted view of world conflict. Most obviously because there are often such 'violations' on both sides. Support for intentional intervention in Libya was bolstered significantly when 'human rights violations' were alleged against the Ghadafi regime. The ICC issued indictments against the Ghadafis in 2011 on the basis of these allegations. The situation became more complicated when similar violations were alleged against the rebels, not least because there was no clear individual for the Courts to indict. When the complexity of conflict is reduced to identifying human rights violations, it inevitably ignores the complexity unfolding on the ground.

In fact, human rights rhetoric encourages moral equivocation. In 2017, a discussion emerged in the UK about whether it was right to kill ISIS fighters on the battlefield or whether it was our obligation under due process to bring them back to the UK to be tried. This followed the killing by drone strike of Sally Jones, a British citizen who had become a known ISIS recruiter. In the aftermath of the killing, a number of human rights supporters argued that our country's 'values', rooted in a commitment to human rights, required that we attempt to try ISIS fighters in our criminal courts. The idea was, presumably, that any individual identified as an ISIS fighter should be forcefully extracted and placed before an English Crown Court.

Many people saw the practical absurdity of the suggestion. But what was interesting about the debate was what it told us about human rights language. Today, human rights rhetoric is used to override notions of citizenship to such an extent, that there is no greater consideration paid to a fellow citizen than there is to someone fighting in a foreign army. There is no difference between the committed jihadist and my next door neighbour. This is a central plank of the human rights argument: that certain qualities of human beings make them automatically immune from particular treatment at the hand of the state. For this minimum standard, it makes no difference whether you are the leader of ISIS committed to ending Western civilisation or a primary school teacher. It also prevents moral consideration of certain courses of action. It is as though there can be no place for revenge or anger in response to ISIS' actions.

A greater irony can be seen in our treatment of those fighting against ISIS. The Terrorist Act lists the Kurdish PKK as a 'proscribed organisation', meaning expressing any support for them amounts to a criminal offence. The PKK have been absolutely central to the West's fight against ISIS in Northern Iraq, yet they remained 'proscribed' largely because of our ties to Turkey through NATO. Our law as it stands extends protections to our enemies while criminalising our allies.

This shows the deep moral confusion engendered by human rights rhetoric. It is perfectly coherent to argue the importance of due process to citizens, to members of our legal and moral community, and to argue that we owe no such duty to foreign fighters. To argue that the question is automatically solved by reference to 'human rights' is avoiding the question rather than answering it. We should be asking why it is wrong to detain terror suspects without charge? Is it wrong to detain all of them in the same way? Is there a difference between those demonstrably fighting for ISIS and those caught up in a terror conspiracy at home? The moral complexity of these questions is bulldozed by a straightforward deference to 'human rights', which does little more than postulate a legalistic answer.

This is why human rights rhetoric gets on the public's nerves. There is an understandable disquiet with our elites appealing to human rights in order to address complex moral questions. Many people legitimately ask why those accused of terror offences cannot be rapidly deported and are frustrated by the answer 'human rights'. They understand that this is not an answer at all. Human rights rhetoric ossifies our moral thinking. It provides us with a route to avoiding the most difficult parts of our moral discussion.

Perhaps there is good reason to hold returning ISIS fighters without charge. Perhaps it is absolutely right to set up a form of internment camp on the UK border where those accused of such offences can be legitimately held without a trial. This may violate everything we think we know about human rights and due process. But so what? Until we explore the moral consequences of these actions, in the most public way possible, the public will continue to resent human rights as allowing moral equivocation on behalf of our decision makers. Those of us who believe in freedom must continue to actively make the case, not equivocate behind the ideologically spent dogma of human rights.

Conclusion

Our recent experience shows us that government responses to terror are far from uniform. They are disparate and unthinking. Recent governments have introduced significant new powers to combat the threat of terror yet many feel less safe than ever before. Many of these powers sit on the statute book unused. While we should all be wary about calls to 'do something' in the face of terror, the alternative of 'coming together' and doing nothing in the face of heinous violence also seems to fall short.

Of course, the interpretation of events is often highly influential in determining the official response. A designation of a particular incident as a 'terror' incident provides calls for further powers with moral force. Similarly, the dismissal of a particular course of action on the basis that it 'violates human rights' ignores the question instead of answering it.

The idea of freedom and security trade off still persists. However, the picture today is more complicated. The powers that have been introduced as a result of terror attacks have not been widely deployed. There is little sense that genuine security has been achieved as a result of recent legislation. To the contrary, it has become increasingly common to believe that the government should be doing more to combat the threat of terror. Where draconian laws do not reflect the reality of policing terror, we are left with powers on the statute books that are unused. The Prevent agenda, which managed to miss the obvious evidence around Salman Abedi while criminalising thousands of innocent Muslims, further illustrates the overwhelmingly disorientated response of the government to the threat of terror.

This climate means freedom is in real jeopardy as well as our security. The belief that more needs to be done to combat Islamism could very easily translate in calls for further draconian laws. The lack of any public agitation in favour of freedom and civil liberty means that any political resistance to such steps is likely to be weak. We need to formulate a response to terror that is unflinching but which is deferential to important freedoms. Our commitment to a sclerotic and aloof human rights regime may well get in the way of formulating the laws we need to deal with today's increasingly complex moral climate.

The Claims of Human Rights Organisations

Today, Human Rights organisations make very grand claims about the power of human rights. The slogan of Amnesty International, 'protect the human' speaks to the simple and unquestioningly noble image they wish to project about their work.

Human Rights lawyers are often thought to be the only good kind of lawyer. In the popular UK film and book franchise Bridget Jones' diary, the eponymous hero's boyfriend is Mark Darcy, a foppish human rights lawyer. The book presents Darcy as the epitome of honest work. While he always tends to work late, the protagonist forgives him on the basis that he is working for a cause greater than himself. The book is a good illustration of how Human rights lawyers enjoy a reputation of selflessness and virtue. If Bridget had fallen for a property or a finance lawyer, it's unlikely she would have been as accommodating to her boyfriend's long hours.

Practising in human rights can also bring high rewards. Recent jurisprudence of the European Court of Human Rights show that human rights cases are not only brought by the 'vulnerable'. A recent case punished a newspaper for publishing the private details of a hedge fund manager's financial arrangements, citing that the newspaper could not rely on article 10 defences[32]. Cases involving Article 10 are regularly bought by the wealthy to protect their reputation from being tarnished in the media. Their purportedly universal application means that human rights don't only serve the rich, but they also don't only service the poor. Barrister's chambers offering human rights work are among the most reputable chambers in the country and offer significant financial recompense for developing a successful practice. Of course, the nature of our justice system is such that those who can afford lawyers are more likely to be afforded protection under human rights laws than those who can't.

Human rights organisations also portray themselves as holding a line against a repeat of historical catastrophe. Central to this is the memory of the holocaust. Proponents of human rights have always presented human rights institutions as an insurance policy against the repeat of previous catastrophes[33]. The campaign by RightsInfo mentioned above, in which visions of the holocaust were interspersed with images of far right rallies in the present day illustrate how the past can be used to justify the work of human rights practitioners in the present.

Human rights groups have a strong influence over contemporary understandings of freedom. When issues around freedom are discussed it tends to be those involved in NGOs surrounding human rights who feature predominantly. Media discussions on issues related to free speech or freedom of association will often feature human rights professionals.

In the UK, websites like Rights Info have been set up explicitly to inform our understanding about human rights, yet they arguably muddy the water further. Under the heading 'what are human rights' their website says they are 'basic moral values which are enforced by law'. They refer to 'values which help keep our society fair, just and equal'. This rather presupposes that we live in a society which is 'fair just and equal' as a result of human rights laws. Had the website been more direct, they may have said human rights, as they exist today, represent a system of laws and institutions which enforce a particular body of law. Appeals to 'values' suggest that contemporary human rights reflect a system of moral norms which are somehow divorced from the institutions that enforce them. As we will see, this significantly over estimates firstly the level of agreement at the level of the European Court of Human Rights as well as the level of agreement at the level of European populaces. This appeal to 'norms' also ignores that moral norms ordinarily arise as a result of public sentiment on a particular issue. The public have no control over the 'norms' established by the judges of the European Court of Human Rights. If the human rights Courts reflect any moral norms at all, it is those propounded by the judiciary rather than those of the European public.

Human rights groups describe the political freedom in entirely legalistic terms. On the website for Amnesty International, under their page regarding freedom of speech, the majority of the page is taken up with a section headed 'when free speech can be restricted'. It claims that freedom of speech comes with 'responsibilities' and lists the circumstances in which the European Court have found it legitimate for a state to place limits on speech. The site's definitions are carefully lifted from the judgements of the ECtHR. For Amnesty, free speech can never be considered an absolute. Its parameters are set by the Strasbourg Court.

Similarly, the website for the campaign group Liberty begins by emphasising the importance of free expression in a 'democratic society' before listing the circumstances in which it can be legitimately limited by the state. These groups are highly influential in public understanding of human rights, but tend to simply regurgitate the wording of the European Court in its public communications. For these organisations, human rights laws are the proper and definitive statement of the extent of particular freedoms.

This legalistic approach to freedom is increasingly evident in education. Students tend to first encounter the idea of liberty in the context of citizenship education. A review of the learning aids available for citizenship classes show that rights are often discussed as being on condition of the exercise of 'responsibilities'. One BBC Bitesize resource includes a page covering 'rights' and states that 'the Universal Decleration of Human Rights' is generally agreed to be a standard for all people in the world to live by'[34] and goes on to describe the passage of human rights law into UK law. These examples are not included to highlight the simplicity of the material's language, but to show that human rights laws have become widely seen as a definitive statement of the extent of our freedom. The words of human rights organisations are given a high place in our debates around our relationship with the state.

We should be more sceptical of the claims of human rights groups. Firstly, human rights organisations dubiously present themselves as part of a historical quest for enlightenment universalism. They often situate themselves alongside great enlightenment thinkers in order to garner moral authority for their project. Secondly, they tend to be unclear or opaque about how the human rights framework made the difference in a particular case. If you look at the detail of the cases, it can be argued that the same result boasted as a 'victory for human rights' could have been achieved using other pre-existing laws. Lastly, pronouncements of human rights organisations are often deeply premature, casting judgements over particular cases which transpire to be inaccurate or misleading. The myths and hyperbole of human rights should be examined and corrected if we are to properly assess the true significance of our human rights framework.

Human rights – trading off history

Today, human rights lawyers draw on the idea of human rights throughout history to justify specific human rights laws in the present. A timeline on the website of Liberty, a leading UK Human Rights campaign group, includes the enactment of the 1998 Human Rights Act as part of the same history as the declarations of the rights of man which followed the French Revolution and the signing of Magna Carta buy king John. The connection drawn between the signing of Magna Carta and the passing of the Human Rights Act suggests that, for Liberty – one of the leading human rights organisations in the country - there is some deep connection between these two pieces of legislation which lift both out of their particular historical context.

Liberty are not alone in drawing the connection between the human rights act and the history of freedom. When New Labour introduced the Human Rights Act, the briefing paper similarly made reference to Magna Carta and claimed that the Act would be 'bringing rights home', a reference to the fact that the freedoms regulated in Europe were born in the UK[35]. Similarly, the Guardian newspaper described the 1998 Act as being '800 years in the making', claiming that the passing of the act meant that the 'process that had begun at Runnymede (with the signing of Magna Carta) had finally reached fruition[36]. The Human Rights Act has always been thought of by its supporters as the end point of a process that has lasted hundreds of years.

Many commentators hold human rights laws responsible for key advances that they actually had nothing to do with. In a 2016 video produced by the Guardian, the actor Patrick Stewart appeared in a sketch playing a fictional Tory Prime Minister on the brink of repealing the Human Rights Act. 'What has the European Convention on Human Rights ever done for us?' he asks. Then his aides chime in. 'Well it ended slavery sir!' says one. 'It granted a right to a fair trial!' said another[37]. The Prime Minister's apparent ignorance of the workings of the Human Rights Act was presumably designed to mirror the misconceptions about the Act that permeate public discussion.

Of course, it was the film itself rather than the fictional prime minister that was confused about human rights. The rights that exist under the European Convention, which had been incorporated into UK law by the Human Rights Act, had arguably existed for millennia before the passing of the European Convention. The 'right to a fair trial' emerged in a melle of English law from around the 18th Century onwards. Every country in Europe had ended slavery by 1956 and the British Empire had not allowed slave labour since 1833. Not even the most fervent supporter of Human rights could legitimately claim that the

European Convention was 'responsible' for these freedoms, or that these were part of what the convention had 'done for us'. However, the short film reflected how human rights supporters are confident in asserting ownership over history.

Human rights organisations have attempted to co-opt the quest for universal morality under the banner of human rights to justify their work. The website for the United Nations Human Rights Office of the High Commissioner says: 'human rights are rights inherent to all human beings, whatever our nationality, place of residence, sex, national or ethnic origin, colour, religion, language, or any other status. We are all equally entitled to our human rights without discrimination. These rights are all interrelated, interdependent and indivisible'. The website for the Equality and Human Rights commission says 'human rights are the basic rights and freedoms that belong to every person in the world, from birth until death. They apply regardless of where you are from, what you believe or how you choose to live your life'. Descriptions of human rights in the material published by prominent human rights organisations all tend to adopt this mystic, internalised idea of how human rights exist and lends strong moral legitimacy to their projects. Ideas of protecting human 'dignity' have been central to the fundraising efforts of key human rights organisations for a long time.

This conception of rights as 'within us' is reflected in recent historical scholarship. Micheline Ishay's book *Human Rights a history from the Ancient to the modern day*[38], argues that the development of human rights thinking can be found throughout all of human history and across an extremely broad range of sources. She defines human rights in terms that emphasise their interiority to human beings and their persistence across history. For Ishay, contributions to human rights came from the Ancient Greeks, Chinese Buddhism, Pre-Christian Judaism right up to the Universal Declaration on Human Rights. They are all part of the same story. Much like the human rights proponents we discussed above, for Ishay, Human Rights have become part of 'who we are'.

Ishay is not alone in claiming that human rights are part of 'who we are'. In her book *Inventing Human Rights*, Lynn Hunt seeks to demonstrate how 'individual minds' contributed to the development of human rights by looking at cultural and societal developments in the 17th – 19th Centuries[39]. Hunt presents an argument that increased capacity for human empathy, stimulated by an increasing interest in literature and public debate through the 18th and 19th centuries led to a greater recognition of certain universal rights. Hunt's focus in on the interior, inherent nature of human rights. Their recognition in law represents an unfolding of our inherent humanity. Our increased capacity to recognise one another as thinking, feeling subjects increased our propensity to think of one another as bearing some breed of inherent right.

Contemporary proponents of human rights also treat them as an ideal to be aspired for, without necessarily accepting the efficacy of any particular human rights legislation. Conor Gearty has defined human rights as the 'phrase that comes to mind when we want to capture in words a particular view of the world that we share with others and we aspire to share with still greater numbers of people'. Gearty acknowledges that specific statues, judicial decisions and bills of rights may well fall short of promoting the 'idea' of human rights. Human rights law represents a step on the 'necessary quest for foundations'[40], a struggle to formulate a universal and permanent human morality which guarantees the 'right of each individual to be treated with as much esteem as any other'. For Gearty, 'human rights' is a term describing humanity's striving for moral universalism.

The idea that human rights are inherent to us explains why the repeal of the Human Rights Act and other human rights laws can come to be seen as an existential threat. If these laws are thought to recognise something deep and universal within all of us, then their repeal suggests a retreat from universalism. This means that human rights laws can be very hard to argue against. If it is believed that human rights are universal and fundamental to being human, criticising human rights institutions becomes a fundamentally anti-human act. Many historians of human rights have identified how human rights stands above the institutions and laws that attempt to realise them. Thinkers like Gearty emphasise that disagreeing or critiquing the operation of one particular human rights instrument should not tarnish the human rights project, or the 'idea' of human rights , which is fundamentally about establishing a basic sense of common decency among all human beings.

There are supporters of the human rights framework who have nonetheless sought to distinguish modern human rights law from the rights fought for in centuries past. Historian Samuel Moyn identifies what he calls the 'continuation fallacy' which suggests that human rights law represent a continuum from enlightenment thinking. For Moyn, who has been openly critical of the work of Ishay and Hunt[41], the vital difference is the role played by the nation state. Rights in revolutionary France or America represented what a citizen would be entitled to do without fear of state interference, as part and parcel of their status as a citizen. Such rights of the 17th and 18th centuries were granted as part of citizenship and statehood. To the contrary, contemporary human rights law represents a transnational restraint on state activity. Rather than an assertion of autonomy on behalf of a citizen, contemporary human rights law allows the citizen to appeal beyond his state to protection from a foreign authority. This marks a clear distinction between the 'droites du homme' of the French revolution or the 'inalienable rights' described by philosophers of the 17th and 18th centuries and the human rights laws of today.

Moyn's work builds on the insight of philosopher Hannah Arendt. Arendt described how the experience of the First World

War illustrated the necessity for new forms of community to guarantee human dignity in a manner that was not dependent on the nation state. The Great War had 'shattered the façade of Europe's political system to lay bare its hidden frame – the sufferings of vast numbers of people to whom the rules of the world around them had suddenly ceased to apply[42]'. Arendt's experience of 'stateless people's led to her believe that 'human rights' – the rights asserted in the course of the revolutions of 17th and 18th Century Europe - were meaningless in the absence of a sovereign nation state who would be willing to recognise and enforce them. The experience of large masses of stateless peoples illustrated that their access to any form of 'dignity' was dependent on their status as a citizen within a political community, a status which in the aftermath of European conflict, many could no longer take for granted.

Arendt's ideas on human rights, which she never developed into a full theory of human rights, is deeply connected to her conception of man as living through productive activity. Arendt describes the condition of man as deeply tied to his capacity to produce meaningful labour in the public sphere. She understood human freedom to be constituted in his ability to undertake productive activity among other human beings, and accordingly to have his capacity to do so respected by any central authority[43]. Freedom was only meaningful in as much it allowed human beings to be productive among other human beings. For this reason, human beings could not be truly free while servicing the basic requirements of their subsistence. True freedom began once the necessities of life had been established and man was meaningfully free to participate in the lives of those around him.

Accordingly, for Arendt, it made little sense to speak of rights which existed 'within us', or without reference to a political community. Without some form of recognition, whether it be from our fellow humans or from some centralised body, rights could be easily violated and rendered meaningless. The stateless peoples of post First World War Europe could not rely on anyone to recognise their freedom, because they were incapable of being objects of recognition at all. What was needed was a new guarantee for human dignity. Arendt never went as far as suggesting a transnational system of human rights law. But for many she illustrated the difficulties in relying on the nation state to enforce the parameters of human dignity in a permanent and transhistorical way, an aspiration that she ascribed to the 'optimistic' nationalism of the 17th and 18th Centuries.

Arendt's important recognition, that rights were effectively meaningless outside of the context of a political community willing to recognise them, has led some to conclude that she should be considered the forerunner of the transnational human rights laws that we have today. But Arendt's philosophy could not account for the heavy influence of realpolitik that influenced the development of human rights law in the mid to late 20th century. Ideas of 'human dignity' and the concept of 'new political communities' would be picked up by elites in the aftermath of the Second World War, in an attempt to provide coherence and moral authority to a collection of deeply divided nations. The aspiration for the architects of human rights was not the universal recognition of 'dignity' as such, although the concept provided a valuable moral veneer to the exercise of political power. Instead, the human rights framework grew out of an attempt to circumvent democracy and undermine the nation state to form new frameworks of transnational government.

When human rights organisations trade on the intellectual legacy of the enlightenment, they disguise how their framework moves away from genuine universalism. Human rights laws are applied by Judges in a selective and sclerotic way. For every person that enjoys a human rights protection under our current human rights laws, another person will be denied. Cases work to narrow the circumstances in which legal protection may be relied upon. This is how the European Court of Human Rights operates. To draw this project into the intellectual history of the enlightenment is to radically overplay the universalising credentials of human rights institutions.

Because the overall impact of human rights laws is so open to critique, human rights groups rely heavily on individual cases with positive outcomes in order to illustrate the importance of human rights laws. A closer consideration of the claims of human rights organisations show that their description of particular human rights laws is often hyperbolic. Human rights organisations can also make claims that are highly politicised. When they are mistaken in their assessment of a particular case, their misjudgements are rarely the subject of comment.

The claims of human rights organisations

In 2016, Liberty launched a campaign called 'Save our Human Rights Act'. This campaign, involving posters and merchandise, listed a number of cases that 'would not have been possible without the human rights act'. The point of the campaign was to encourage the idea that human rights represent a small part of our justice system that genuinely cares about vulnerable people. The term 'our' Human Rights Act also suggested that this piece of legislation belonged to the public rather than those in power. It was something we owned in order to limit the power of the state[44].

The campaign material was hyperbolic about the impact of the Human Rights Act. The campaign proclaimed:

'Our Human Rights Act has already achieved so much. It's held the State to account for spying on us, safeguarded our soldiers, and supported peaceful protest. It's helped rape victims, defended domestic violence sufferers, and guarded against slavery. It's protected those in care, shielded press freedom, and provided answers for grieving families. Its protections are the most fundamental – those we should all enjoy, because we're human'.

It was as though Liberty had drawn up a list of people widely considered to be the most vulnerable in society and claimed that the Human Rights Act had helped them on that basis alone.

These claims are very broad. Firstly, the term 'held the state to account' is vague. The Human Rights Act has not figured at all in the passage of key pieces of legislation which increased the state's ability to 'spy' on us. As we have seen, the claim that the Act had 'shielded press freedom' ignores the fact that the Act has been on the statute book at a time when freedom of the press has been subject to significant limitation by our government. The Levenson Inquiry sought to establish the first statutory regulator of the press for centuries. Human rights laws simply do not appear in the significant debates around press freedom. An argument could be made that a case under the Act had allowed for a defence of a particular kind of press freedom for a particular journalist under particular circumstances. A good example is the case of *Financial Times and Others v United Kingdom*[45] which narrowly prevented the disclosure of journalistic sources in the course of UK litigation on the basis that it would violate Article 10. But this is not 'shielding press freedom', but rather deciding that a particular violation of press freedom is unacceptable, while allowing a multitude of others. The leading authorities involving the United Kingdom and Article 10 involve the justification on limits on press freedom, as we will see in a later chapter. The claim that the Act had 'guarded against slavery' was not questioned, even though slavery has been illegal throughout the British empire since the early 19th Century.

Along with the hyperbolic written materials, Liberty produced a series of videos in which high profile actors told the stories of those who had experienced victories under the Human Rights Act. The actors delivered short recordings of the claimant's perspective on the case and pleaded with people to donate and become involved in their campaign.

The stories were designed to elicit an emotional response

to a particular piece of legislation. The focus on 'stories' and personalised accounts were deployed to emphasise the importance of the Act. Specifics as to the broader application of the Act did not feature in the campaign. Instead, the focus was on the emotional impact that particular outcomes had had on those effected. While these were touching, they provided little insight into how exactly the Act was influential in a particular case.

Deepcut

The deaths at Deepcut Barracks came to public attention during 2002. James Collinson was a 17 year old soldier from Perth. On the evening of 23rd March 2002, his body was found in the grounds of the Officers' Mess at the Princess Royal Barracks, Deepcut, near Camberley in Surrey. He had suffered a single gunshot wound to his chin. The army, along with members of his family, concluded that this was either a suicide or a prank gone badly wrong. But this was not the end of the story. Collinson was the fourth trainee to die in similar circumstances since 1995. Privates Geoff Gray, Sean Benton and Cheryl James had all reportedly killed themselves while on guard duty at the same barracks[46].

Collinson's death was investigated by both the civilian and military police forces. Surrey Police were the civilian police force in charge of the criminal investigation. The job of this investigation was to establish whether there was any evidence of homicide and whether there was any evidence that would assist the coroner in determining how Collinson had died. The civilian investigation was the first to be carried out with respect to the deaths at Deepcut. The investigations into the previous deaths had all been carried out by the Royal Military Police alone. In the course of investigating Collinson's death, Surrey police concluded that investigations should be reopened into the death of Geoff Gray. Later, in July, investigations were reopened into the deaths of Sean Benton and Cheryl James[47].

By 2003, four police reports had been completed. The investigations had accumulated a huge amount of information. Surrey police had taken 1500 witness statement and commissioned their own independent forensic analysis of exhibits and key ballistic evidence. The reports concluded with respect to each soldier that there was no evidence of any third-party involvement in any of the deaths at Deepcut. It was this new material, the 1500 witness statements, which would eventually become the subject of interventions by human rights organisations later on.

The material gathered by Surrey Police had been obtained further to a criminal investigation into the deaths. Now that there would be no criminal proceedings arising from the investigation, the material obtained by the police was considered to be confidential.

In September 2003 the new reports were presented to the coroner dealing with the Inquest into Collinson's death. He had to consider, firstly, whether there was anything in the reports into Collinson's death which would assist him in determining the cause. He would also have to consider whether the reports into the previous deaths justified reopening the 'very brief' proceedings that had recorded open verdicts. In October, the coroner wrote to the soldiers' families to explain that, in his view, the material gathered in the course of the civilian investigation did not justify reopening the inquests into the deaths of the three soldiers.

By September 2003, it was clear that Surrey police were considering far more than just whether or not anyone had killed any of the four soldiers. They had taken on an investigative role that went well beyond what would ordinarily assist a coroner. Their investigation into Deepcut became about the conditions at the barracks which may have led the soldiers to take their own lives. By 2004, Surrey police had published a report identifying that 'evidence of (bullying) behaviour has been uncovered in sufficient quantity to raise concerns'. The investigations into

Deepcut became a wide-ranging investigation into the culture at the barracks, which went beyond the ranks of Surrey police. The House of Commons Defence Select Committee decided to conduct an inquiry of its own into duty of care regimes in training establishments across all three services of the armed forces[48].

The family of Cheryl James were understandably unsatisfied with the verdicts of the previous inquest. They suspected she had been raped and sexually assaulted by her fellow soldiers and that this had been a key contributing factor to her death. They believed that some of the evidence gathered by Surrey police's investigation would support such a claim. They instructed Liberty to lobby for a fresh inquest. On the 'threat of litigation', Surrey police disclosed additional material to Liberty relating to the initial Inquest. These documents, including '44 volumes of statements, documents, notes and photographs[49]' - raised doubts about the credibility of some of the evidence received in the original inquest. In July 2014, the High Court ordered a fresh inquest which would consider further evidence about the circumstances leading to James' death.

Preliminary hearings at the new Inquest ruled that it would be empowered to consider whether there had been any evidence supportive of the claim that James herself had been sexually attacked prior to her death, but not evidence regarding a 'culture' of sexual abuse at Deepcut[50].In January 2016, Alison Foster QC told a pre-inquest hearing that the new material suggested James may have been sexually coerced or raped the night before or before the time of her death and a direct allegation that James may have been ordered to sleep with a person superior in rank.

Liberty said that it was the 'threat of action' under the Human Rights Act that compelled the police to disclose the material which led to the new inquest. Their lawyers remarked that the Act was central to forcing a new Inquest to take place. But the detail on what Liberty did and how they used the Act was unclear. It may well be that the police disclosed the files following the 'threat' of action. But the Act itself does not contain any provision to compel a public body to disclose material. The fact that Liberty pointed to the 'threat' of action is indicative that no action was ever actually taken under the Act. We do not know whether, in due course, the Act would have made any substantive difference to the case.

The first question that should be asked is whether a new inquest could have happened without the Act. The answer to that is plainly yes. Firstly, it is worth noting that in 2009 the provisions of the Human Rights Act effectively came to be included in the Coroners and Justice Act of 2009. Section 5 of that Act details the 'matters to be ascertained' by the coroner's investigation. Parliament could easily have included a provision that widened the ambit of a coroner's investigation to mirror the requirements of the Convention. In fact, section 5 2 effectively does this by saying: 'where necessary in order to avoid a breach of any Convention rights (within the meaning of the Human Rights Act 1998 (c. 42)), the purpose mentioned in subsection (1) (b) is to be read as including the purpose of ascertaining in what circumstances the deceased came by his or her death'. The fact that the Act was used to 'threaten' litigation is hardly a ringing endorsement of its power to enforce transparency.

It is beyond doubt that the Human Rights Act widened the ambit of what fell to be considered during an inquest. This is because European Court of Human Rights jurisprudence set certain requirements that an Inquest had to abide by in order to be compliant with the convention. Prior to the passing of the Human Rights Act, Inquests were concerned with establishing 'how, when and where' a person had died. The ambit of the investigation was restricted to 'by what means', rather than 'in what broad circumstances' a person had met their death. A number of possible verdicts were available including unlawful killing, misadventure right through to industrial disease.

After the passing of the Human Rights Act, a number of authorities established that Inquests had to go further than this to ensure compliance with Article 2. This included a requirement that the next-of-kin of the deceased must be involved in the inquiry to the extent necessary to safeguard their legitimate interests. It was this newly widened ambit that gave new impetus to calls to reopen the original inquests.

But the impact of this expanded remit was largely therapeutic. The article 2 jurisprudence made clear that it was vital, in the words of the Lord Chancellor and the Court of Appeal, that participation in the proceedings provide grieving families with 'peace of mind'. In this new remit, the job of the Inquest becomes providing family members with closure and emotional relief.

This raises issues about the balance between the need for families to achieve closure and the interests of the institution under investigation. In the Deepcut case, there is no doubt that the cause of James' death was a single gunshot wound inflicted by herself. The reasons that she killed herself are undoubtedly complex and her family have an entirely legitimate interest in investigating. But this must be balanced with the integrity of the institution, as well as the interests of other soldiers who may have been involved. Prioritising the 'peace of mind' of a grieving family over the ability of the army to maintain confidentiality is not necessarily beneficial. Perhaps Deepcut will be a unique case. But the real risk is that it sets a precedent for lengthy inquests into similar cases in which therapeutic closure becomes the paramount concern. This is not necessarily a good thing for the army or its soldiers.

The introduction of the Human Rights Act did not dramatically increase the powers of the coroner's Court. It did not make the tribunal better able to establish the truth. In fact, as the UK charity Inquest make clear, the state's processes around dealing with deaths at the hand of the state are still woeful in many situations. What it did do was require the Inquest to involve a grieving family to a greater extent.

This raises a further serious question about what people should expect from a public body. Do we really want Inquests to resolve questions of *why* someone may have taken their own life? The idea of a state body undertaking such an investigation is at least double edged. If the Inquest concludes that the culture at Deepcut played no part in James' death, should we accept that verdict as gospel? Why should one family be entitled to such a judicially sanctioned investigation and another not? On its own terms, no one would say that granting a new Inquest into these deaths is a bad thing. But it raises a problem: should it really be the job of an Inquest to establish the reasons that someone took their own life?

Liberty's use of this case does not demonstrate that the Human Rights Act ensures justice or better adherence to due process. The Human Rights Act did not do anything that ordinary statute law could not have done. The fact that the case for the Human Rights Act in the context of Inquest proceedings is made on the back of suffering, and the attempt by the law to alleviate or 'provide peace of mind' to amend that suffering, suggests that the power of the Act is more emotive than practical. It has done little to improve the processes involved with Inquests. It has merely given the appearance of a more caring and compassionate state. Meanwhile, the real problems around state accountability for individual deaths remain.

Christopher Alder

The second case put forward by Liberty is that of Christopher Alder. Christopher died in April, 1998 while in police custody. He had been injured in a scuffle while on a night out. He had been taken to hospital, but was then arrested for breach of the peace and taken to the police station. He died on the floor of a police cell by choking on his own vomit, while officers around him stood around chatting and laughing. Video footage of the moments leading up to Christopher's death emerged in which the officers can be heard to make monkey noises as he died.

In 1999, 5 officers were charged in connection with Chris' death. A jury at Chris' inquest held that he had been unlawfully killed, but a criminal trial in 2002 concluded with the Judge throwing the case out due to lack of evidence. In 2004, the Home Secretary David Blunkett ordered an investigation by the IPCC into the case.

Liberty and the family took the UK government to the European Court of Human Rights. They alleged that Christopher's treatment amounted to breaches of Christopher's right to life. They also alleged that there had been a failure by the state to properly investigate the case.

The government then took the almost unprecedented step of settling the case with Alder's family, offering them 23,000 Euros in compensation plus their legal costs. The settlement came with an apology, which said there had not been an effective and independent investigation into the death.

Undoubtedly, the government's actions in paying out compensation were completely right. Christopher's treatment was utterly appalling and his family deserved justice.

However, two points are worth noting about Liberty's use of this case to illustrate the importance of the Human Rights Act. Firstly, Alder's case is the exception rather than the rule. Figures from Inquest suggest between 32 and 45 people have died in police custody in the course of the last 3 years[51]. Alder's is one of very few to have received an apology and compensation. Of course, this is not because more people lack access to human rights lawyers. It is because in order to receive any kind of remedy under human rights laws you have to have a very particular set of circumstances. For every Chris Alder there are many more deaths in police custody that will not be acknowledged by the narrow terms of our human rights laws.

Secondly, the European Court of Human Rights didn't have

any real involvement or impact in the case. They simply ruled the case admissible. This is hardly remarkable. We do not know whether the case would have been successful had the final judgement been delivered, nor on what terms the case might have succeeded. For all we know, the Human Rights Act may have completely failed the Alder family eventually. It was only because the government settled that we are able to call this a victory. There may have been a multitude of reasons for the government settling that had nothing to do with the strength of the claim.

This is all the more prescient when we consider the recent decision of the Court in *Armani Da Silva v UK*, which dealt with the circumstances surrounding the death of Jean Charles de Menezes. This leaves real room for doubt as to whether the European Court of Human Rights would have found in the Alder family's favour. De Menezes was an innocent man who was gunned down on the London underground by anti-terror police on the basis of misinformation and police incompetence. In Armani Da Silva, the Court concluded that the mere lack of any prosecution with respect to any particular officers in De Menezes' case was not sufficient to argue that there had not been an investigation compliant with Article 1. The Court also accepted that the evidential test applied by the CPS in deciding whether to prosecute, had been within the State's discretion (the state's "margin of appreciation") to decide on such matters. Without further clarification, there is nothing to say that the case of Alder is sufficiently different from Armani Da Silva to suggest that the Court would have decided for the family.

We will probably never know why the government finally settled in Alder's case. In any event, and notwithstanding detailed findings of guilt, it is absolutely right that Alder's family received an apology and compensation. The fact that the individual officers were not prosecuted does not retract from the responsibility of the state as a whole for Alder's death. But to use this case as an example of the vitality of the Human Rights Act ignores the fact that the Human Rights Act was not tested in the context of Alder's case. Recent Strasbourg jurisprudence suggests it may not have helped. We have no way of knowing whether the Court would have eventually supported the family or not.

Modern Slavery

Modern slavery is a significant issue in contemporary human rights discussion. Liberty's website discusses the case of Patience:

Patience was brought to the United Kingdom as a domestic worker and a nanny. For two-and-a-half years, she was abused physically and mentally. She was never paid, or given time off, and her employer withheld her passport. Eventually, with the help of a neighbour, Patience managed to escape – only to be confronted with an uninterested police force, refusing to take any of her allegations seriously. No effective investigation was carried out, and Patience's employer was not even interviewed.

Thanks to Article 4 of our Human Rights Act (sic), no slavery or forced labour, officers were forced to investigate on Patience's behalf, and her employer was eventually prosecuted – although not for slavery or forced servitude, as they still were not offences under English law.

Recent evidence suggests that Patience was far from alone when it came to police inaction in the face of these offences. A 2017 report claimed that police were 'failing to handle' modern slavery claims. The report found evidence that the police were closing investigations early and failing to properly identify victims[52].

The difference between slavery that was abolished across the British Empire in 1833 and 'modern slavery' is the role of the state. A vital element of slavery's evil was the state's endorsement of property rights over people. The fact that you could legally own another human being is what made slavery historically specific.

The problem with modern slavery is that it can be very difficult to distinguish between a criminal offence and simply unusual working conditions. Evidence often involves workplaces where someone present has alleged conditions of slavery. Other people working at the same place may claim that they are working for payment. Payment for ad hoc work can often be paid in cash, so if an employer suggests such payments were made it could be difficult to corroborate an allegation of unpaid work. If police officers show up to a haulage yard in which someone claims they are working as a slave, but the other persons present disagree with that evidence, it is difficult to see what the police can do to build a case on the basis of their word alone.

With regards to Patience, we are not given the specifics of her case. It is difficult to assess any apparent failure. But one thing is clear: police officers cannot investigate anything which is not a criminal offence. Because they were able to investigate something with respect to Patience, albeit not slavery, there must have been a crime committed. Let's assume it is the 'abuse' that the website identifies. The police did not investigate this 'because of' Article 4 of the European Convention on Human Rights. They were always under an obligation to investigate subject to the evidence being available. The Human Rights Act does not contain any power to compel the police to do a job they are already supposed to do. Liberty's presentation of this case imbues the Act with a mythical power it does not contain.

The Act is also given credit for political advances it had nothing to do with. The website continues: 'Thankfully…there is a new modern slavery offence now on the statute book – thanks in part to our Human Rights Act'. It is not clear how Liberty claim that the Act compelled the passing of new legislation. This is especially true given that the new Anti-Slavery Act was passed largely thanks to Theresa May, hardly someone to be guided by the provisions of the Human Rights Act.

Russia – rushing to judgement

Russia is among the European Court of Human Rights' most prolific offenders. It is the country with the third most cases decided against it, behind Turkey and Italy. Around a third of cases lodged with the Court are against Russia. A review of the case law reveals that often, the Court is involved in chastising the Russian state for obvious failings in the treatment of people under the care or detention of the state[53]. The Court orders damages which will probably never be paid. In as much as these judgments make a difference to individual claimants, they should be welcomed as a corrective to the frequent bad behaviour of Russian state authorities.

However, the treatment of Russia by the European Court of Human Rights and associated NGOs is not always positive. Human rights organisations are deeply unpopular within Russia. In the ongoing conflict between the Court, Human rights NGOs and the Russian state, Putin has presented himself as a robust defender of the country's conservative values. The Court has come to be seen as a foreign eloper, dictating values from above, and chastising the Russian courts for failing to fall in line.

Human rights organisations have also politicised high profile cases involving Russia without good cause. A good example is the case of Mikhail Khodorkovsky. Khodorkovsky was once thought to be the richest man in Russia. He was an oil tycoon and head of Yukos, one of the country's largest oil companies. Yukos was depended on by millions of Russians for energy. Such was the significance of Yukos in Russian society that Khodorkovsky was often visited by Vladimir Putin to discuss what he could do to make the company›s work easier.

Khodorkovsky was arrested in 2003 following allegations of wide spread fraud and tax evasion during his management of the company. His business partner, Platon Lebedev had been arrested previously on similar charges. The Russian state set about seizing Yukos assets and their share price plummeted. As one of Russia's largest private oil companies, this led to huge numbers of investors losing huge sums of money. Many within Russia thought the arrest was politically motivated and that Vladimir Putin was seeking to bring the large company under control.

While the Court proceedings against Yukos and Khodorkovsky continued, the European Human Rights community identified the case as suitable for intervention. In 2005, the Council heard the report of Sabine Leuthesser-Scharrenberger, who had been commissioned by the council to report on the case. The report had been compiled following two visits by Leutheusser-Scharrenberger to Moscow, during which she questioned members of the official prosecutor's office about the case, as well as interviewing various human rights NGOs and 'retired judges'. On the basis of these visits, she concluded that there were 'serious corroborated shortcomings' in the prosecution of Yukos. She described to the Council how Russia had amended its tax laws in 2004 and that Yukos had been prosecuted retrospectively under the new law. They were the only company to be prosecuted under the new law, suggesting they had been singled out due to their size. Members of the council, on hearing the report, agreed that while it was important 'not to prejudge the outcome of any later investigation' that there appeared to be strong evidence that the prosecution was 'political'[54]. In October 2007, the Parliamentary Assembly at the Council of Europe passed a resolution to monitor the trial for ongoing procedural unfairness.

Leutheusser-Schnarrenberger continued to offer statements of support to Khodorkovsky. She denounced his trial as unfair and even claimed that what he had been accused of did not amount to serious criminality. In 2009 she said 'I would dispute any sweeping statement that everything Mr. Khodorkovsky is accused of can be generally judged criminal. Some of the acts were performed by everyone, and legal at the time'. A prominent member of the European Council was claiming that the alleged tax evasion undertaken by Khodorkovsky was not particularly serious. It is hard to imagine how the UK authorities would react were a similar approach to be taken in response to a domestic prosecution for evading UK taxes[55].

The council produced further reports on the case, claiming with even more brazen language that a 'privately owned oil company, (had been) made bankrupt and broken up for the benefit of the state owned company'. It alleged that the Russian state had effectively commandeered Yukos at the expense not only of Yukos shareholders but also the Russian public who depended heavily on the company. They went on to say that the Russian state had bought back the assets it had seized from Yukos at a reduced price effectively mirroring the behaviour that it had alleged against Yukos. For the Council of Europe, Khodorkovsky became a powerful symbol of the tension between human rights standards and the Russian state. It continued to consciously take sides against Russia, hosting Russian human rights activists at conferences in which Khodorkovsky was held up as an example of an ongoing assault by the Russian state on civil society.

Amnesty International also threw their oar behind Khodorkovsky. In 2011, in the course of a widely publicised report into the case, the organisation 'declared' Khodorkovsky and his business partner to be ‹prisoners of conscience›. ‹Whatever the rights and wrongs of Mikhail Khodorkovsky and Platon Lebedev's first convictions there can no longer be any doubt that their second trial was deeply flawed and politically motivated[56]," said Nicola Duckworth, Amnesty International's Director for Europe and Central Asia. She continued to indict the lower Court system in Russia, saying "for several years now these two men have been trapped in a judicial vortex that answers to political not legal considerations. Today's verdict makes it clear that Russia's lower courts are unable, or unwilling, to deliver justice in their cases."

These were strong words from Amnesty. Duckworth was effectively accusing the entire lower Court system of Russia of systemic corruption. Again, it is hard to imagine how the UK government would react if a Russian monitoring group questioned the functioning of Her Majesty's Revenue and Customs or the First Tier Tax Tribunal in the same way.

Western MPs also felt confident in proclaiming the political nature of Khodorkovsky's imprisonment. In a parliamentary debate in 2013, Conservative MP Richard Ottaway encouraged MPs to remember, "Mikhail Khodorkovsky, the former head of the Yukos oil company, who fell out with the Kremlin after challenging official corruption. He is currently serving his 10th year in a prison cell, on grounds that are distinctly flaky and based on a trial that did not comply with the standards that we would recognise in the west." Support for Khodorkovsky crossed the benches. Labour MP Kerry McArthy said the case showed how ‹human rights standards› were ‹experiencing a clampdown in contemporary Russia›[57].

The international human rights community rushed to make judgements about the Khodorkovsky case almost immediately following his arrest. The idea that Russia had effectively changed the law slowly to take control of Yukos became mainstream. When the feminist band Pussy Riot were arrested comparisons were drawn between the band and the collapsed oil company, both being considered as symptoms of a deep disregard of the rule of law in Russia.

However, the European Court of Human Rights did not see it this way. The shareholders of Yukos lodged a complaint with the Court alleging that the treatment of the company had unfairly deprived them of property, that Yukos had been denied the right to a fair trial and that the Russian state had violated the convention against discrimination by prosecuting Yukos and not any other oil company. The case provided by the shareholders implicitly alleged that the company had been singled out by the Kremlin and denied the right to defend itself. At the same time as launching the human rights case, investors sought to take action through various national arbitration Courts across Europe, using the rules of international trade to claim that the Russians had acted unlawfully.

In a judgement delivered in September 2011, just months after Duckworth and Amnesty International declared the men to be 'prisoners of conscience', the European Court of Human Rights found that there was no evidence that the prosecution of the men had been political. In fact, in reading the judgements of the lower Courts, they had found that Yukos had behaved unlawfully in seeking to evade Russian taxes. The Court said that the assessments of tax, interest and penalties were in accordance with the laws of Russia, reasonably foreseeable, and that Yukos had failed to prove that the application of those laws to Yukos was either discriminatory or motivated by a collateral political purpose.

The Court did not let Russia off the hook. They found instead that various aspects of the process involved in prosecuting the men and seizing the company assets had breached the articles of the convention. They had not been given sufficient time to prepare their case with respect to explaining the company's tax affairs. The assessment of the company's tax liabilities and the subsequent doubling of the same liabilities was found to be unlawful. The Court's decisions on the lawfulness of the tax assessments was split four votes to three. Yet, they unanimously rejected the claim that Yukos had been treated differently than any other company would have been in the circumstances. The European Court made an unprecedented order for damages in the sum of 1.9 billion Euros against the Russian state that was to be paid to Yukos shareholders.

The decision in the Yukos case followed years of Khodorkovsky being used as a symbol of human rights abuses in Russia. But the reality was inevitably more complex. The Russian system of dealing with tax evasion may well have been patently unfair. But how does it compare to other countries? In the UK, defendants in tax cases can now be subject to civil orders depriving them of property, restraint orders which can prevent them disposing of any of their assets and blocking all of their bank accounts. Companies can be made bankrupt by the powers of Her Majesty's Revenue and Customs. Now the National Crime Agency is similarly granted powers over investigating tax debts. Of course, our system is fairer than Russia's. But painting Russia's dealings with Yukos as an egregious violation of human rights may well be calling the kettle black. Khodorkovsky's case shows how human rights institutions can be more concerned with generating mythology than in impartially assessing particular circumstances.

The European Court of Human Rights v UK
Connor Gearty is one of our leading thinkers on human rights. His work is essential reading for anyone who wants to understand how human rights work. His latest book, *On Fantasy Island* betrays his political leanings as an ardent anti-Breixteer. However, there are few other thinkers in the UK who can explain the mechanisms of the Act and the Judges who apply it more clearly. However, a review of the cases he discusses demonstrates the need to situate cases in their political context. When we view the impact of the Human Rights Act solely from the perspective of law, we can lose sight of the problems that persist in spite of apparently progressive judgements. This is the danger inherent in relying on human rights laws, or buying into the human rights propaganda. We become oblivious to the significant inroads into freedom that these cases represent. We will see in the cases that follow, human rights can be used to give a moral sheen to the overreach of state power.

The first is the case of interest is *Chahal v United Kingdom*. Chahal was a Sikh separatist. Since the partition of India in 1947, Sikh separatists had been fighting for a separate state in Northern

India. On two occasions during the 1980s Chahal had been detained on suspicion of being involved in plot to assassinate the Indian prime minister. On both occasions he was released without charge. In March 1986 he was charged with assault and affray following disturbances at the East Ham gurdwara in London. During the course of his trial on these charges in May 1987 there was a disturbance at the Belvedere gurdwara, which was widely reported in the national press. Chahal was arrested in connection with this incident and was brought to Court in handcuffs. All of his convictions were eventually quashed because the UK Court of Appeal found that bringing him to Court in handcuffs rendered his trial unfair.

When a journalist went to see Chahal in 1995, he gave the following description:

'Amid the drab surroundings of the visitors' meeting room at Bedford prison, inmate HD2167 presents an exotic spectacle. He stands to greet visitors, a massively bearded and turbaned figure wearing traditional kurtha pyjamas - long flapping white shirt and baggy trousers. As he bows and shakes hands in polite salutation, it is hard not to feel that he looks seriously out of place. Karamjit Singh Chahal has been looking out of place for some time now. Five years and one month to be precise. "Every day I ask myself, 'Why am I here?'" he says as he sits down at the bare table.'

The reason Chahal was incarcerated was our backwards terror laws. Despite never being convicted of any terror offences, the then Home Secretary decided that Mr Chahal ought to be deported because his continued presence in the United Kingdom was 'unconducive to the public good for reasons of national security' and 'other reasons of a political nature', namely the international fight against terrorism. Chahal claimed that if returned to India he had a well-founded fear of persecution within the terms of the United Nations 1951 Convention on the Status of Refugees ("the 1951 Convention") because of his associations with Sikh separatism, albeit it that he strenuously denied any involvement in terrorist activity. He applied for political asylum. The European Court of Human Rights eventually ruled that his deportation would violate his Article 3 right in that he faced a real risk of torture and inhumane treatment were he to be returned to India.

Chahal is commonly cited as an authority for the proposition that Article 3 is an absolute prohibition against torture, inhumane and degrading treatment. For Gearty, this case shows how the Human Rights Act compels the Courts to take fairness and due process seriously. Gearty's point is that the Article forces the Court to treat Chahal with respect notwithstanding his status as an alleged terrorist. However, Gearty ignores another argument that was made in Chahal which dealt with the circumstances of his detention. It is the treatment of this argument which shows how dangerous our contemporary reliance on human rights laws can be.

Chahal maintained that his detention had ceased to be "in accordance with a procedure prescribed by law" for the purposes of Article 5 para. 1 (art. 5-1) because of its excessive duration. By the time his case reached the European Court of Human Rights he had been detained for 6 years. The Court pointed out that all that was required for the detention to be justified under article 5 (1) is that "action (was) being taken with a view to deportation". As long as the proceedings were being brought with 'due diligence' then the detention will be permissible. It was also immaterial, for the purposes of Article 5 para. 1, whether the underlying decision to expel could be justified under national or Convention law. So even though someone's eventual deportation may be unlawful under the convention, they could still be held pending the resolution of their case.

For Gearty, the message we should take from Chahal is that the Human Rights Act gives voice to even the most unsympathetic of people. But look at it another way: Chahal was locked up for 6 years without being safely convicted of an offence. On heavily disputed evidence, he was held without any charge while the UK government decided whether it was legal to deport him. The opportunity Mr Chahal was given to have his voice heard was in front of an advisory panel, at which he was not entitled to a lawyer and was not given any of the evidence against him. He was allowed to call witnesses on his behalf but was not to be informed of the advice which the panel gave to the Home Secretary.

You could take Chahal as evidence that Human Rights are indiscriminate in their protection. Or you could take Chahal's case as showing how human rights protections are fundamentally performative. As long as the state 'takes action' pursuant to deportation, then Article 5 will not bite. As long as the government goes through the motions of reviewing a particular case then detention without charge is entirely legitimate, even when the process of review is farcical. The Court even noted that the advisory panel did not constitute a 'Court' for the purposes of Article 6, so the state's obligations for a fair trial did not apply. It is at best a narrow interpretation of this case to say that it gave voice to the voiceless when the voice was entirely neutered by state power.

A similar point can be made about the other case mentioned by Gearty, *HL v United Kingdom*. HL concerned an autistic adult who had been admitted into hospital as an informal patient. This meant he lacked the capacity to decide where he wanted to stay. The European Court found that the lack of procedural safeguards around the treatment of HL meant that he was deprived of his liberty in violation of article 5. Gearty credits the European Court with compelling our mental health institutions to respect the rights of patients. Yet, he does not consider any evidence about the impact of these 'procedural safeguards'. Instead, he asserts, rather than substantively argues, that their introduction was a benefit to those it purported to protect.

The judgement in HL led to the introduction of Deprivation of Liberty Safeguards in the 2009 Mental Capacity Act. This made it harder to keep people in hospital on an informal basis where care staff considered it was in their best interests. Later research suggested that care staff began looking for excuses not to have to seek authorisation for a 'deprivation of liberty' under the act. Where they did, lawyers often became involved in decision making which only tended to make things more complex. According to research published in 2011, disagreements about whether a given set of conditions amounted to a deprivation of liberty were 'most pronounced among...eminent lawyers'. I am not saying that these safeguards actively made things worse. No doubt there are plenty of people out there better qualified to say than me. But neither should we blindly assume that 'procedural safeguards' in and of themselves make a situation better. These 'safeguards' are checks and balances on professional judgement. Lawyers like to imagine that they are uniquely placed to know what is best for someone. When it comes to these 'procedural safeguards', it is worth thinking carefully about how they impact on the work that psychiatric professionals do, rather than merely celebrating the recognition of people's rights as such.

Many of the high profile cases involving the UK involve asylum and deportation. These cases have included findings that a claim by two ex-employees of the UN could not rely on Article 8 to prevent their deportation back to Afghanistan even if they faced ill treatment by the Taliban. The Court found that the men had failed to provide evidence to prove that their personal circumstances would expose them to a real risk of inhuman or degrading treatment if removed. Their work for the international community had not been high profile and there was nothing to prove that the Taliban had the motivation or ability to pursue low level collaborators in Kabul, an area outside of Taliban control. Another failed asylum seeker received short shrift from the Court after claiming that his status as an amputee meant his deportation would amount to ill treatment. With a few notable exceptions[58], cases involving the UK and its immigration and asylum policy tend to be found against the applicant[59]. Where they went with the applicant, the case found a narrow violation[60] or required the applicant to show a real and immediate threat to their lives were they to be deported. Even the most vociferous supporters of human rights would struggle to claim that these judgements, most of which go against the applicants, have radically improved the lives of immigrants and asylum seekers in the UK.

It is only once you review the significant authorities emerging from the European court of Human Rights, which we will continue to do in the chapters to come, that you come to see that we have little to lose from leaving its remit. The Court's judgements do little to change the trajectory of anti-freedom law in the UK. It does little to curb even the most draconian areas of the UK legal system. The Court certainly prides itself on promoting a set of 'values'. But its impact on the development of the law around significant political freedoms has been minimal. It does nothing to solve the complex moral questions posed by migrants or asylum seekers. The very idea that we stand to return to a 'perceived idyll of the 1930s' if we left the Court's remit radically overstates its function. The use of this kind of language is a moral equivocation. It reflects a reluctance to deal with the political questions that the human rights courts can never solve on our behalf.

It is precisely because the real impact of the Act has been so minimal at the level of legal authority that human rights organisations have to defer to the 'threat' of legislation to prove its impact. This is why they have to focus on the emotional impact of particular cases, to focus in tightly on individual stories, rather than discussing the narrow legal remit that the Act exerts. In our discussion on human rights, we have to see through the claims of human rights organisations to see what the Act really does. Only then will we see that we have little to lose from its repeal.

Conclusion

Human rights laws propagate two key myths. On the one hand, they falsely convince us that we live in a society where individual rights are respected. An examination of the decisions involving immigration and terror suspects only serve to undermine the claim that human rights laws are universally applicable. Human rights supporters tend to believe that the existence of such laws should always trump the interests of our community. This is why the Human Rights Act is often deployed to challenge the authority of our institutions. The fact that such challenges can be made is treated by human rights supporters as a good thing in itself. But we need to weigh the balance between a respect for individual rights and the interests of wider society. We should assess these laws in their context. Human rights proponents are too often happy to celebrate human rights laws without considering their impact on wider society and the institutions that purport to defend our common interests.

It is dangerous that human rights have developed a mythical status in Western society, particularly in Britain. They are presented by their supporters as the latest moment in humanity's journey towards universalism. This perspective prevents a consideration of human rights laws in their particular social and political context. Human rights organisations add to the problem by generating a narrative around human rights that exaggerates their utility. Accounts as to why human rights laws work are often based on individual accounts and emotive stories, which tell us little about how particular laws actually made a difference in a particular case. The reality is that human rights laws protect a narrow and deeply qualified idea of freedom. They defend the idea that judges should set the parameters for how free we should be. They do this on the basis that leaving freedom to be determined by democracy will inevitably lead to tyranny or genocide.

The Judiciary's democratic mandate

In 2008, one of the UK leading Judges, Tom Bingham, said that the Human Rights Act had given the Judiciary a 'democratic mandate' to adjudicate over the boundaries of political freedom[61]. Bingham was absolutely right. The Human Rights Act placed the Judiciary in the role of deciding how freedoms should be balanced. How they undertake this task is the subject of this chapter,

Today, the term 'human rights' has developed a very broad remit. If you look at the websites for most human rights institutions, you could be excused for believing that 'human rights' have been responsible for every political advance in human civilisation. The civil rights movement in America, the end of slavery, the drafting of Magna Carta and the passing of the human rights act have all been cited as examples of 'human rights' influence on history.

Human rights organisations also identify 'human rights issues' in all sorts of contemporary problems. Following the appalling tragedy at Grenfell Tower, in which 71 people died during a fire in a North London tower block, the website Rights Info produced a video explaining why Grenfell Tower was a 'human rights issue' in virtue of the fact that the people in the tower had had their 'right to life' violated. This was not technically incorrect. Plainly the victims of Grenfell had had their right to life interfered with, in as much as they had been killed while in Council accommodation. But to call Grenfell Tower a 'human rights issue' drained it of political content. It imagined the tragedy at Grenfell as a mass violation of individual rights, rather than a symptom of a complex political problem affecting a community. It was an individualised and legalistic way of conceiving of an appalling event.

Today, 'human rights issue' is almost synonymous with

the term 'political issue'. Many cases which begin as political movements, such as the campaign to legalise assisted suicide in the UK, end up as human rights cases once the political campaign is thought to be exhausted. This process was described by Neil Stammers as the 'paradox of institutionalisation' at the heart of contemporary discussions about human rights. By relying on the machinery of the state in the form of human rights laws to challenge state power, social movements become unable to effect change within state bodies without the assistance of the state itself[62]. Often, the case itself becomes the end to which the campaign is geared.

In this climate, Judges can find themselves adjudicating on all kinds of cases which are capable of being described as political. Of course, this does not mean that the Judge will necessarily make a politicised decision. But the decision will have a political impact. In recent years, the growth of Judicial Review has meant that Judges have been able to quash the decisions of elected ministers. The growth of law around decision making in public bodies mean that more decisions taken by those bodies are vulnerable to judicial intervention. The Human Rights Act has introduced a new mechanism through which the Judiciary can assess, challenge and undermine policies and decisions made by elected representatives.

Qualified rights, qualified freedoms

The first thing you learn at law school about the European Convention is that it contains both 'absolute' and 'qualified' rights. Absolute rights, the Convention states, are protected without qualification. They include the right to life (Article 2) prohibition on torture (Article 3). 'Qualified right' means that a state can 'interfere' with the right, but only within the terms allowed for by the convention. Essentially, it is the Judges of the UK Upper Courts and the European Court of Human Rights that decide how we as citizens are able to use that right. Through precedent, the Court establishes when and how someone will be able to rely on their rights under the Convention.

Qualified rights under the convention can be split into two parts. First, Article's protecting qualified rights set out the nature of the right protected. They then set out the circumstances in which those rights can be lawfully interfered with. States can be found to have 'interfered' with a convention right, but a case will only be successful if a state is found in 'violation' of the Convention, by interfering beyond the grounds allowed for by the terms of the relevant article. Take for example article 10 which relates to freedom of expression:

Everyone has the right to freedom of expression. This right shall include freedom to hold opinions and to receive and impart information and ideas without interference by public authority and regardless of frontiers. This Article shall not prevent States from requiring the licensing of broadcasting, television or cinema enterprises.

The article then goes on to say:

'The exercise of these freedoms, since it carries with it duties and responsibilities, may be subject to such formalities, conditions, restrictions or penalties as are prescribed by law and are necessary in a democratic society, in the interests of national security, territorial integrity or public safety, for the prevention of disorder or crime, for the protection of health or morals, for the protection of the reputation or rights of others, for preventing the disclosure of information received in confidence, or for maintaining the authority and impartiality of the judiciary'

The wording of this Article suggests that freedom of speech under article 10 is a deeply 'qualified' right. The Articles reference to 'limitations' 'formalities, conditions, restrictions or penalties' that can lawfully be imposed on a person's freedom of expression anticipates a very wide set of circumstances in which freedom of speech can be lawfully interfered with under the convention.

Where a right is 'qualified' the Court has to decide whether the interference with a right amounts to a 'violation' of the Convention. The state will only violate the Convention if it fails to meet the two prong test. First, the legal rule in question must be accessible to the individual. This is known as the publicity or 'accessibility of law' requirement. The law must be formulated with precision as to its meaning and scope. This is described as the foreseeability of the law requirement. The most important step, and the one in which the Court most often finds a violation, is the test of 'democratic necessity' – that is, whether the interference was 'necessary in a democratic society' or whether there was a 'pressing social need' for the law – in which the Court turns to a proper assessment of the justificatory grounds provided by the State Party.

The fact that the Court is often called on to decide what is 'necessary in a 'democratic society' means it is often engaged in fundamentally political judgements. It politically assesses the steps taken by member states to regulate qualified rights. This often involves considering other areas of the countries' policies to assess whether a particular decision or policy is truly 'necessary' in the context of that state's legal system. This has led to significant divergences in standards. The 'democratic society' test has given rise to broad inconsistency in applying Article 10. It has led the Court to treat different countries differently. Put simply, you are far more likely to have your case considered a violation of the Convention if you live in Russia or Turkey, than you are if you live in the UK or France.

The UK is given a very wide 'margin of appreciation' to determine the proper ambit of article 10 for itself. This means that cases involving apparent interferences with free speech can be rubber stamped by the European Court without considering the substance of the complaint. A recent case brought by Paul Gough, the naked rambler, was dismissed because of the significant margin of appreciation granted to the UK to determine how to regulate public nudity. The fact that the European Court of Human Rights have rarely got involved in the UK's decisions around free speech means much of the decisions regarding the ambit of Article 10 emerge from the senior UK Courts.

In order to determine how Human Rights laws protect our freedom, it is therefore necessary to consider the judgements in significant cases. The UK case of Animal Defenders v UK illustrated the House of Lords' reasoning around freedom of speech and Article 10. The case focused on the ban on political advertising in the UK. This case was brought by an animal rights campaign group who argued that the ban interfered with their rights to freedom of expression. They had wanted to publish an advert called 'my mates a primate', in which a chimp pictured inside a cage would gradually transform into a 4 year old girl. The advert pointed to the fact that chimps have a 'mental age' of a four year old. The advert was submitted to the Broadcast Advertising Clearance Centre, who declined to authorise the advert because it was 'wholly or mainly political in nature' and therefore breached the provisions of the 2003 Communications Act. They argued that in being prevented from broadcasting the ad, their article 10 rights had been infringed.

Animal Defenders International went to the High Court to argue that the ban on political advertising was incompatible with human rights law. They sought a 'declaration of incompatibility' from the High Courts which would have had the effect of forcing parliament to reconsider the law that enforced the ban. The Animal Defenders case was fundamentally political. The declaration would have meant that the government would have had to consider amending or repealing the ban entirely. In calling for such a declaration, Animal defenders were seeking to directly undermine the authority of a democratically elected law through a declaration that its provisions were incompatible with the European Convention on Human Rights.

The UK House of Lords found that the advertising ban did interfere with the applicant's freedom of expression. The advert was certainly a form of political expression. The parties also agreed in advance that the violation was 'prescribed by law' and that it responded to a legitimate need to protect the rights of minority political causes. The only question that was considered at length by the Court was whether or not the ban was 'necessary in a democratic society'.

Lord Bingham gave the lead judgement in the case. Bingham was deferential to the power of parliament to understand what was required of democracy. He said that MPs would be 'particularly well attuned' to what was required to facilitate democratic debate. He also noted that parliament had considered the implications of article 10 when drafting the law around the ban and had decided to proceed anyway. This, he said, was something which should not be 'lightly overridden'. Bingham was echoing a common sentiment among the UK Judiciary, which encourages deference to parliament as the elected chamber.

However, his judgement also included some of his own ideas about why free speech was important and how it should be protected. Some of Bingham's reasoning adopted a classical liberal position, not completely out of step with John Stuart Mill:

28. The fundamental rationale of the democratic process is that if competing views, opinions and policies are publicly debated and exposed to public scrutiny the good will over time drive out the bad and the true prevail over the false. It must be assumed that, given time, the public will make a sound choice when, in the course of the democratic process, it has the right to choose. But it is highly desirable that the playing field of debate should be so far as practicable level.

This is achieved where, in public discussion, differing views are expressed, contradicted, answered and debated. It is the duty of broadcasters to achieve this object in an impartial way by presenting balanced programmes in which all lawful views may be ventilated."

It's hard to disagree with any of this. But Bingham continues:

"...well-endowed interests which are not political parties are able to use the power of the purse to give enhanced prominence to views which may be true or false, attractive to progressive minds or unattractive, beneficial or injurious. *The risk is that objects which are essentially political may come to be accepted by the public not because they are shown in public debate to be right but because, by dint of constant repetition, the public has been conditioned to accept them.* The rights of others which a restriction on the exercise of the right to free expression may properly be designed to protect must, in my judgment, include a right to be protected against the potential mischief of partial political advertising."

This was a small insight into Bingham's reasoning for upholding the advertising ban. He considered the ban important because of a risk that the public would be 'conditioned' to accept arguments by 'dint of constant recognition'. Bingham thought the ban was necessary to avoid organisations with 'objectionable goals'. The Court claimed that it was particularly important to regulate broadcast media because radio and television was 'more persuasive' for the general public than other forums.

In considering this judgement, it is worth distinguishing between its legal coherence and its political and normative assumptions. Legally, the decision is meticulous and logical as you would expect from a senior Judge. However, what I would call 'the political content' of the judgement, the passages in which Bingham makes normative judgements about the scope of freedom of speech, is deeply open to question. These are fundamentally questions about our view of human beings. Is it really correct that people come to accept arguments simply by 'dint of constant repetition?' Are people really susceptible to advertising in the manner that Bingham suggests? You might agree with him, you might not. But this is a political assumption about the nature of human judgement, made by a single Judge sat in the House of Lords. There is no reason to suspect that Thomas Bingham has any better insight on this particular question than anyone else.

It is in these small moments that Judges veer into, what I think can sensibly be called, 'political' judgements. Of course, Judges in senior Courts have to draw on their experiences when deciding certain facts. But in these cases, Judges are required to make decisions about how society should balance important freedoms. Here, Lord Bingham was being asked to decide how society should control the ebb and flow of public discussion. Whatever you think of his decision, this was something which did not fit clearly into legal expertise. This was not the fault of Lord Bingham. He did not ask to make this decision. But the case is illustrative of how human rights laws can oblige Judges to reach beyond their judicial and legal expertise to make judgements about how we should treat political freedoms.

Adopting Bingham's idea about the importance of free speech to prevent the public being won over 'by dint of constant repetition' could have adverse political consequences. Conceiving of the public as susceptible to such 'conditioning' arguably leaves freedom of speech open to further interference. All sorts of restrictions of freedom of expression are justifiable if you proceed on the basis that the public are constantly susceptible to malign influences. Indeed, this has been the intellectual foreground to censorship for hundreds of years. Bingham's description of certain groups as 'objectionable' raises further political questions. Why should the state be the arbiter of who is 'objectionable' and who is legitimate in a democratic public debate? Bingham's conception of free speech is arguably one built on the logic of censorship, which encourages the idea that the public are easily controlled by the media they encounter. Of course, Bingham has no power to pass statutory law. But this argument could just as quickly be used by those seeking to undermine free speech as those who seek to protect it.

The European Court of Human Rights endorsed the findings of the UK Courts and Animal Defenders International's case was dismissed. In one respect, this was a good outcome. It is an indication of the Court's deference to democratically determined law that they refused to interfere with a ban introduced by statute. However, at the same time, the judgement leaves space for questions. In a society whose ideas about freedom are significantly influenced by legal institutions, there is a real danger that the remarks of Tom Bingham about the susceptible nature of the British public become part of our political understanding of freedom of speech. Bingham's judgement could, in the future, provide the impetus for further censorship on the basis that the public need protecting from 'objectionable ideas'.

Article 10 has also had an impact on the freedom of the press. In 2004, the model Naomi Campbell brought litigation against the Daily Mirror newspaper for publishing articles alleging that she had a serious drug problem and was attending rehab. She obtained an injunction and sought damages against the paper. By the time the case reached the House of Lords, both sides accepted that there had been a violation of the newspaper's right to free expression. Again, the only question was whether this interference was 'necessary in a democratic society'.

Campbell's lawyers accepted that the reports regarding their client's drug problems were legitimate, because Campbell had claimed in the public eye that she did not have a drug problem. The publication of these facts were 'necessary to correct a false impression' created by Campbell. However, the paper had gone further than that. They had published further details about the model's engagement with treatment. They had published photographs taken covertly of Campbell entering and leaving her treatment. The publication of the additional material justified the intervention of the Courts, argued Campbell's lawyers. The fact that the photographs were taken covertly and deliberately with a view to publication and the lack of any compelling need for the public to have the additional information, the public interest already being satisfied by the publication of the core facts of her addition and treatment. Campbell won the case. As well as damages to Campbell, the newspaper had been ordered to pay 1,086,296.47.

The House of Lords considered three cases from the European Court of Human Rights, which they said gave them the 'principles' they needed to adjudicate on Campbell's case. Lord Hope found that there was no doubt that the choices made about the presentation of material that was legitimate to convey to the public was pre-eminently an editorial matter with which the court would not interfere. However, 'the public interest in disclosing private material had to be balanced against the right of the individual to respect for their private life: those decisions were open to review by the court'.

Hope went on to conclude that while there was a clear public interest in correcting Ms Campbell's impression, given by her, that she was not taking drugs, there was no concurrent public interest in knowing the details of her treatment.

Again, it is in this 'balancing' of different freedoms that Judges inevitably become involved in political considerations. These are questions connected to the kind of society we want to live in. These two cases, which remain authoritative on the proper application of article 10 in the UK, shows how the Human Rights Act has placed power in the hands of Judges to decide the extent of particular freedoms, or in their words, to 'balance them' against one another. The question we face when considering the human rights act repeal is not whether we want to be 'dragged to a perceived idyll of the 1930s', but whether we want the Judiciary to retain the power to make these important political decisions on the scope of political freedom.

Article 5 and detention without charge

Other articles containing qualified rights mirror the structure of article 10. Article 5, protects the right to liberty and security. Again the article begins with the words 'everyone has the right to liberty and security of person'. The article then goes on to state the terms on which people can be legitimately deprived of their liberty and security. It says:

> No one shall be deprived of his liberty save in the following cases and in accordance with a procedure prescribed by law:
>
> (a) the lawful detention of a person after conviction by a competent court;
>
> (b) the lawful arrest or detention of a person for noncompliance with the lawful order of a court or in order to secure the fulfilment of any obligation prescribed by law; 8 9
>
> (c) the lawful arrest or detention of a person effected for the purpose of bringing him before the competent legal authority on reasonable suspicion of having committed an offence or when it is reasonably considered necessary to prevent his committing an offence or fleeing after having done so; (d) the detention of a minor by lawful order for the purpose of educational supervision or his lawful detention for the purpose of bringing him before the competent legal authority;
>
> (e) the lawful detention of persons for the prevention of the spreading of infectious diseases, of persons of unsound mind, alcoholics or drug addicts or vagrants; (f) the lawful arrest or detention of a person to prevent his effecting an unauthorised entry into the country or of a person against whom action is

being taken with a view to deportation or extradition

Plainly, the article anticipates a wide range of circumstances in which a person's right to liberty and security can be interfered with. Today, the UK has the longest period of pre-charge detention compared with any other democracy. Other European countries allow for detention without charge, but for significantly shorter periods of time. France have provisions to detain people for four days, Germany for two days, Greece for six days, Norway for two days, and Spain for five days. Even though other countries in Europe arguably face a greater threat from Islamist terrorism, given their shared land border with countries bordering the Middle East, our laws grant the greatest power to the police to detain pre-charge.

There is no evidence that the increased powers have allowed for the more effective investigation of terrorism offences. In a case study involving a wide scale plot to blow up aeroplanes, the police were unable to demonstrate that the powers to detain persons for 28 days had made any difference to their ability to investigate. There was no correlation between the length of time someone was kept in custody and the likelihood of their being charged. Those who were kept in custody the longest, in one case for 27 days and 20 hours, had been released without charge while most of those who were charged in the conspiracy were charged within 2 days of arrest. It appears that prolonged periods of detention without charge do not make the police better at tackling terrorist plots.

While it has developed in scope during recent decades, detention without charge in the UK is not new. Since the 1971 Immigration Act, the Secretary of State has been able to detain any non-British National 'pending the making of a deportation order against him'. This means that any immigrant who is subject to deportation proceedings can be held in immigration detention while their case is considered. The Courts in the UK have ruled that the power under that Act only lasted for as long as was 'reasonably necessary' for the process of deportation to be carried out but in practice this placed little limit on the amount of time immigrants could be expected to be detained for. Figures published in 2014 showed that immigrants had been detained for up to 1518 days under these powers, all of which has been found to be perfectly legitimate under the European Convention.

In fact, as we have seen in the case of Chahal above, the European Court of Human Rights has indicated that as long as something is being done to action an immigrant's deportation, a state will be largely free to detain the person for as long as necessary. They have said repeatedly that 'any deprivation of liberty under Article 5 § 1 (f) will be justified only for as long as deportation proceedings are in progress. If such proceedings are not prosecuted with due diligence, the detention will cease to be permissible"[63]. There is no fixed definition of due diligence.

Further, the European Court of Human Rights has ruled that the UK law around immigration detention is perfectly compliant with article 5. In a recent case, the parties submitted that the system of immigration detention was not sufficiently clear or precise and gave detainees no idea how long they stood to be held in custody for. The European Court of Human Rights pointed out that they had rejected this argument 'despite the absence of fixed time-limits and/or automatic judicial review, the system of immigration detention was sufficiently accessible, precise and foreseeable in its application because it permitted the detainee to challenge the lawfulness and Convention compliance of his ongoing detention at any time'. In other words, because the detainee was able to challenge the lawfulness of the detention the law was sufficiently clear.

Immigrants are not the only people who the British State can lawfully hold without charge. Those accused of terrorism have never really felt the benefit of the Convention, which gives considerable leverage to states – especially states like the UK – to decide how they should respond to the threat of terrorism. Take the example of Ireland. As we mentioned previously, the European Convention on Human Rights did absolutely nothing to prevent the appalling violations of civil liberties against Irish Catholics during their conflict with the United Kingdom. Of course, this is hardly surprising. While Thatcher's government famously denied that the UK was at war with the Irish Republican movement, many on both sides of the Irish Sea could see that the UK was treating the Irish catholic population as a hostile entity. But the case of Ireland highlights the ongoing hypocrisy of human rights legislation and its role in providing symbolic rather than substantive protections over important democratic freedoms.

The Irish case is an example of how states have been able to 'derogate' from their obligations under the convention in cases of 'national emergency'. In 1961, the European Court heard the case of Mr Lawless, who was challenging his detention in the Republic of Ireland. Lawless was a self-professed member of the IRA. He was detained in a military prison in July 1957 and detained without being charged. In August 1957, Lawless was told that he could be released if he signed an undertaking agreeing 'to respect the Constitution and laws of Ireland' and not to 'be a member of or assist any organisation which is an unlawful organisation under the Offences against the State Act, 1939.' He refused to sign. Instead, he challenged the lawfulness of his detention, firstly to the European Commission on Human Rights and later to the European Court of Human Rights.

Prior to detaining Lawless, the Irish government had taken steps under Article 15 of the European Convention, which allowed for the derogation from its obligations under the Convention at times of national emergency. Derogations allow for states to suspend their obligations under the convention under certain circumstances. In effect, the State can temporarily withdraw from its obligations in order to respond to a particular circumstance. Article 15 says:

> In a time of war or other public emergency threatening the life of the nation any High Contracting Party may take measures derogating from its obligations under this Convention to the extent strictly required by the exigencies of the situation, provided that such measures are not inconsistent with its other obligations under international law

The European Court found that the threat of Irish republicanism constituted an 'emergency' threatening the life of the nation' which meant it could lawfully 'derogate' from its obligations under the convention and continue to detain Lawless without charging him. The Commission accepted that his detention violated his right to liberty and security, but was legitimate because the Irish government had lawfully derogated from its obligations. In a later case, the European Court found that states would be granted a 'wide margin of appreciation' as to when to derogate from the Convention, meaning it would be reluctant to intervene when a state had decided to derogate based on the state's belief that it faced an 'emergency threatening the life of the nation'.

The use of derogations to pursue detention without charge was deployed by New Labour following 9/11. In the months following the terrorist atrocities in New York, they began by immediately issuing a 'derogation order' under Article 15, much like the Irish had done prior to the Lawless case. The UK claimed that there 'existed a terrorist threat to the United Kingdom from persons suspected of involvement in international terrorism' following the 9/11 attacks and therefore sought to derogate from its normal responsibilities under article 5 of the convention.

After issuing the derogation order, Labour passed the 2001 Anti-Terrorism Crime and Security Act which allowed any foreign national suspected of terrorism offences to be detained indefinitely. The Act was a complete affront. Civil liberties groups reminded the New Labour government that indefinite detention without charge was completely contrary to ancient principles of justice.

This led to the first big test for Article 5, in the Belmarsh case. In 2005 a group of nine detainees at Belmarsh prison, who were being held under the indefinite detention provisions of the 2001 Act, challenged their detention. The men were terror suspects who allegedly belonged to a range of terrorist organisations. The case reached the House of Lords.

The House of Lords had traditionally kept out of cases involving national security. Since the Second World War, a number of decisions had demonstrated their unwillingness to become involved in deciding about matters that they thought better resolved by the government of the day. One decision of the House of Lords in 1985 described national security as 'par excellence a non-justiciable question' with another saying it was 'clearly a matter for executive discretion and nothing else'.

The issue of whether the Court should intervene in what was an apparently political question was raised in argument in the Belmarsh case. The Attorney general sought to persuade the Court that the determination of what was necessary in response to 9/11 was a matter for the government. He argued that the Court was constituted of Judges who were unelected and that judicial authority required 'proper limits'. Thomas Bingham responded that Judges had been given, by the Human Rights Act, a democratic mandate to '(delineate) the boundaries of a rights-based democracy'. Bingham's point was that the Human Rights Act represented a democratic mandate for Judges to decide questions which may appear, on their, face to be political because they involved the boundaries of legally enforced rights. The judgement represented a judiciary willing to assert greater authority over issues which previously had been the preserve of the executive.

The Judges eventually declared the men's detention to be unlawful under the Human Rights Act because it violated their rights under article 5 of the European Convention. But this was not because their detention was wrong in principle. The Judges held that the system of incarceration without trial was not 'strictly required' within the meaning of article 15 and so went beyond what the government was lawfully capable of under their derogation. The sections of the Act which allowed for indefinite detention were disproportionate because they did not rationally address the threat to the security of the UK presented by Al-Qaeda terrorists specifically. The provisions did not, the Court found, address the threat presented by UK terror suspects while allowing for the detention of persons who were not suspected of presenting any threat to the security of the UK as Al-Qaeda terrorists or supporters.

Human rights organisations welcomed the judgement as a watershed moment for human rights in the UK. One academic described it as 'perhaps the most powerful judicial defence of liberty" since the 1770s and hoped that that it "will long remain a benchmark in public law". The case was widely conceived of as an example of the House of Lords being willing to stand up for freedom in the face of an apparently draconian government. The case is still celebrated by human rights organisations as a landmark decision which confirmed the significance of the human rights act in the struggle for civil liberties.

However, there are a couple of reasons to doubt the status of the Belmarsh case as a 'powerful judicial defence of liberty'. Firstly, the Judges were not considering the question of whether detention without charge was right or wrong, or whether the decision to issue the derogation order was politically acceptable thing to do. The Court was considering the far narrower question of proportionality, with particular reference to discrimination. It is widely thought that the reason why the Judges fell in favour of the men was because the law was discriminatory, not because detention without charge was wrong in principle. The question that vexed the Court had nothing to do with 'liberty'. Instead, they were focused on whether the measure was proportionate. As legal writer Jon Holbrook has said, 'The House of Lords (in the Belmarsh case) came close to holding that an erosion of civil liberties would be tolerated so long as the erosion was non-discriminatory'.

Secondly, Belmarsh has proven not to be the benchmark that some have thought it could be. Cases since the Belmarsh case have tended towards allowing greater deference to elected governments in determining matters of national security. It seems there is a limit to the Judiciary's willingness to limit the more draconian elements of state activity.

With the above caveats, it is right to say that the Belmarsh case did have an immediate impact on the law. The Court ordered a 'quashing order' against the derogation order. They also issued a declaration under section 4 of the Human Rights Act 1998 that section 23 of the Anti-terrorism, Crime and Security Act 2001 was incompatible with articles 5 and 14 of the European Convention.

In light of the Judgement, the government were forced to rethink its approach to detention without charge. However, the outcome was the introduction of control orders in the Prevention of Terrorism Act of 2006. Control orders allowed for suspects to effectively be put under house arrest. Boundaries could be placed around suspects' homes that they were not permitted to cross. They could be prevented from using the telephone and from interacting with particular people. The Act also allowed for terror suspects to be detained without charge initially for 28 days. Article 5 certainly had an impact on the law around detention without charge, but it did relatively little to rein in the draconian instincts of new labour when dealing with terror suspects.

While the Belmarsh case had an impact on the law around

detention without charge, its effect has not been significant. The government were able to craft a new regime around the terms of the judgement. It gave a judicial seal of approval to the framework of anti-terror laws that still persist in a moderated form to this day.

A recent European Court case highlights how the new regime around detention without charge manages to remain human rights compliant while bordering on the Kafkaesque. Sher and his co-defendants were arrested on the 8th of April 2009 on suspicion of being involved in the commission and institution of acts of terrorism. They were held without charge in police custody until the 21st of April, a total of 13 days. On the 21st of April they were 'released' without charge, before being placed immediately into the custody of immigration services. They were served with deportation notices[64].

Their initial detention had been authorised under schedule 8 of the 2000 Terrorism Act. Sher's case was that their detention violated articles 4 and 5 of the convention, because they were not given sufficient specific information about the allegations against them to challenge their ongoing detention. They also complained that much of the proceedings were held in private and that the state should have appointed a 'special advocate' to represent their interests. Finally they argued that the warrants deployed to search their homes were so widely drawn that they violated their rights under Article 8, which protects their private and family life.

The European Court of Human Rights found that any complaint that the men's article 4 or 5 rights had been violated was 'inadmissible' because they had not 'exhausted domestic remedies'. The Court found that the men could have brought a private case against the police from Pakistan in the UK Courts. The claimants pointed out that they were in Pakistan with no access to legal aid and insufficient money to bring a private law case. The government argued that they had nonetheless failed to prove that legal aid was impossible to obtain. The European Court agreed with the government and concluded that the complaint about article and 5 was inadmissible, largely because the applicants had not proven what the government already knew: that it would be impossible for them to get legal aid to fund a private law challenge.

The rule regarding domestic remedies is a good thing for state sovereignty. The Court is deferential to domestic Courts to the extent that they won't interfere where domestic Courts can correct problems themselves. But it is also a procedural pitfall which, in cases like this, can lead to complaints being inadmissible merely because the applicants have not taken completely academic steps, like applying for legal aid in cases where it is bound to be refused.

The applicants went on to argue that they were entitled to be represented by a special advocate in the closed sessions that considered their detention. The government disagreed, and argued that the procedures that were followed were in accordance with Schedule 8 of the Terrorism Act. The European Court of Human Rights found no violation of Article 5. The Court said that terrorist crime falls into a 'special category' and that the detailed procedures of Schedule 8 provided sufficient safeguards to a defendant's interests:

A detained person must be given notice of an application for a warrant of further detention and details of the grounds upon which further detention is sought. He is entitled to legal representation at the hearing and has the right to make written or oral submissions. The possibility of withholding specified information from the detained person and his lawyer is likewise provided for in Schedule 8 and is subject to the court's authorisation. Schedule 8 also sets out the right of the court to order that a detained person and his lawyer be excluded from any part of a hearing.

While these procedural safeguards may sound reassuring, they are in practice largely performative. A District Judge in a Magistrates' Court is highly unlikely to order the release of a terror suspect where a senior police officer is claiming that a terror attack is 'imminent', even if the claim is unsupported by direct evidence. Much evidence in terrorism cases is likely to be circumstantial, in the form of phone calls or other forms of association. This requires an explanation from a defendant, but often as here the defendant lacks the information required to mount a defence. In any event, a defendant in any criminal proceedings should not be forced to give an account of themselves in advance in order to secure his release. Providing a defence in advance of seeing the entirety of the case against you is suicide in a criminal trial, because it leaves a defendant vulnerable to criticism over the smallest inconsistency. A defendant in schedule 8 proceedings would be foolhardy to offer any kind of case in response to the evidence against him and may even be denied the information and representation in order to make such a defence possible. These procedures do not provide a realistic opportunity for a defendant to secure his release, yet their existence works to legitimise detention without charge under our human rights regime.

Conclusion

The Human Rights Act has allowed the Judiciary to become involved in regulating the parameters of important civil liberties. Their protection of these liberties has been extremely limited. The European Court of Human Rights does not prevent violations of civil liberties. It decides when such violations can be held to be in violation of the European Convention on Human Rights. It decides which breaches, or 'interferences' in the Court's language, can be justified within the terms of the convention. They have to decide whether an interference in a person's rights are 'necessary in a democratic society'. This inevitably means they become involved in fundamentally political questions about what a state has to do to avoid punishment for breaching fundamental freedoms. Yet, as recent case law shows, often the procedural steps that have to be taken by a state to pass muster with the European Court of Human Rights are largely performative. A state just has to go through the motions and all sorts of severely draconian measures will be considered entirely justified. For this reason, our human rights framework provides an entirely baseless protection against state encroachment. It provides an illusory freedom.

Conclusion

The fear of freedom

While we apparently live in a 'hegemony of human rights'[65], support for freedom is in crisis. Across the Western world, traditional political freedoms are struggling to maintain their significance. In a striking survey publicised by the New York Times Sunday review, research showed that only about 30 percent of Americans born after 1980 believe it is absolutely essential to live in a democratic country, compared with 72 percent of Americans born before World War II. In 1995, 16 percent of Americans in their late teens and early adulthood thought democracy was a bad idea; in 2011, the number increased to 24 percent.

The survey also revealed that young Americans also are disproportionately sceptical of free speech. A 2015 poll from the Pew Research Centre found that 40 percent of millennials (ages 18 to 34) believe the government should be able to regulate certain types of offensive speech. Only 27 percent of Gen-Xers (ages 35 to 50), 20 percent of baby boomers (ages 51 to 69) and 12 percent of the silent generation (ages 70 to 87) share that opinion[66].

The mounting rejection of free speech is easily observable when you look at Western universities. In the UK and the USA, student movements have rebranded free speech as a tool for 'fascists'. During one highly publicised incident at the US Evergreen College, students blockaded their teachers in University buildings after certain faculty members refused to abide by a 'no white' day on campus. One staff member went on Fox news about the protest, saying that it typified the appalling attitude that many students hold towards free speech[67]. This staff member received significant backlash from the student population who claimed his adherence to free speech values was placing other students in danger. Recent research has shown that almost every university campus in the UK has at least some limit on what can and cannot be said on campus[68]. Many have blanket 'no platform policies' which prevent speakers with certain views speaking to students.

These speech codes are enforced by a vocal minority of students. In 2017, a survey of 3,000 college students by Gallup for the Knight Foundation and the Newseum Institute found that 78% favour campuses where offensive and biased speech is permitted. A separate study found that even at Yale 72% oppose codes that circumscribe speech, compared with 16% in favour. What the survey referred to as 'illiberal tendencies' were limited to about 20% of college students.

Yet this 20 percent have a real impact on what other people on campus think they can say. At Yale, 42% of students (and 71% of conservatives) say they feel uncomfortable giving their opinions on politics, race, religion and gender. Self-censorship becomes more common as students progress through university: 61% of freshmen feel comfortable speaking freely about their views, but the same is true of just 56% of sophomores and 49% of juniors[69].

There has also been some major institutional changes. In 2017, the American Civil Liberties Union 'revised' its position on free speech following popular backlash for its support of the right of the far right to protest. This was a significant development. The ACLU gained significant prominence for defending the rights of fascists to speak freely. The ACLU says on its website that its defence of the first amendment is 'unequivocal'. They famously defended the rights of a Nazi organisation to march through the Jewish neighbourhood of Stoke Illinois during the 1970s. It has been the most prominent defender of free speech for the last 100 years.

Yet this unqualified position became compromised in 2017. The ACLU sued the town of Charlottesville to allow far right demonstrators to march there. The suit was successful and the march went ahead as planned. It was widely reported. Protestors marched with tikitki torches chanting 'you will not replace us'. Following clashes with left wing protestors, one protestor was killed. The US president Donald Trump was heavily criticised for claiming that there were 'bad people' on both sides of the demonstration.

At first, the ACLU held strong for their defence of the right to protest, despite the claims that they were in some sense accountable for the protestor's death. In a statement the ACLU executive director Anthony Romero insisted hateful, bigoted speech must be aired. "Racism and bigotry will not be eradicated if we merely force them underground," Romero wrote. "Equality and justice will only be achieved if society looks such bigotry squarely in the eyes and renounces it." It appeared that the ACLU would hold the line for the rights of fascists to march.

Yet the pressure on the ACLU to change its position remained strong. Virginia Governor Terry McAuliffe, levelled blame at the ACLU for the resulting violence. "The city of Charlottesville asked for that (protest) to be moved out of downtown Charlottesville to a park about a mile and a half away -- a lot of open fields," McAuliffe. "That was the place that it should've been. We were, unfortunately, sued by the ACLU. And the judge ruled against us." One columnist penned a piece said the ACLU needed to 'rethink its stance' on free speech in the name of protecting minority rights. One senior staff member resigned saying he would not be a 'fig leaf for fascists'. An open letter was penned by junior staff members asking that the organisation retreat from its 'unequivocal' position.

The suggestion of the backlash against the ACLU was that it was their protection of the rights of protestors that led to the violence. The ACLU had 'blood on its hands' according to one comment piece. The idea that those organisations who defend freedom of speech can then be blamed for the appalling act of individuals has become increasingly common.

The ACLU and Charlottesville incident also showcased another depressing fact about contemporary freedom in the West. The various incarnations of the far-right have dominated our discussions on free speech in recent years. Whenever free speech makes the headlines, it is because of the curtailment of certain rights afforded to 'far right' or otherwise uninteresting speakers. Milo Yiannopoulos, an internet troll, hosted a 'Free Speech week' event at Berkley University which caught national headlines after it was violently protested by left wing groups. The designation of free speech as a 'tool of the far right' has benefitted those like Yiaanoplous, who paint themselves as warriors of free speech against the forces of left wing censorship.

Free speech has come to be seen as a pretext for violence and disorder. This is, after all, one of the most popular arguments for censorship that has persisted throughout history. All regimes in the past have justified repressive laws and draconian attacks on civil liberties on the basis of some kind of protection.

Human rights discourse is now starting to contribute to this climate. In November 2017, a Canadian graduate student called Lindsay Shepherd received a complaint for using a clip of Jordan Peterson in her teaching. Peterson is a prominent Canadian social commentator, who has become controversial because of his views on transgenderism. Shepherd was told that her use of the clip in her teaching violated bill C16 of the Canadian Human Rights code which added gender identity and gender expression to the list of prohibited grounds of discrimination. Canadian human rights laws were used to justify limits on academic freedom and freedom of discussion. Today, students in the UK and the US cite the 'right to feel safe' as a justification for limiting free speech on campus.

In Europe, the rights of religious minorities continue to be undermined, with the support of human rights laws. In 2010, the French government banned face coverings making it illegal for anyone to wear anything covering their face in public. While the law applied to balaclavas and other face coverings, the law was widely considered to be targeting Muslim women. In 2009, President Nicholas Sarkozy had said "We cannot accept to have in our country women who are prisoners behind netting, cut off from all social life, deprived of identity. That is not the idea that the French republic has of women's dignity. The burqa is not a sign of religion, it is a sign of subservience. It will not be welcome on the territory of the French republic."

A 24 year old Pakistani national brought a case to the European Court of Human Rights. Lawyers for the applicant argued that the ban was 'inhumane and degrading, against the right of respect for family and private life, freedom of thought, conscience and religion, freedom of speech and discriminatory"

The Court did not agree. It found that the law was proportionate and addressed the aim of the French government to allow people to 'live together'. The rights of minorities in this case did not trump the right of the French state to decide for itself how to legislate face covering.

The burqa ban decision was arguably a victory for democracy. It showed that the Court understood that the law reflected a conflict in French society that had to be resolved in the political rather than the legal sphere. But the case must leave a bad taste in the mouth of human rights supporters. The judgement also shows how the Universalist aspirations of the Court place it in conflict with democracy. The Burqa Ban decision was largely seen as anomalous in the context of the Strasbourg Court. Its supporters were quick to describe the decision as out of step with the universal protection of minority rights that the Court aspires to. It were as though the Court had failed in correcting the 'backward' view of the French people. The surprise at the Burqa ban decision reflected how the Court is expected to wade in to complicated political questions and bestow an answer from on high. Across Europe, support for freedom is collapsing. If we are to resist the gradual erosion of significant political freedoms, we have to start convincing people that political freedom is important. The Burqa case shows that we cannot depend on our human rights courts to instil the kind of culture we need for freedom to flourish.

What are we afraid of?

In our legalistic age, it has become hard for us to think of freedom without human rights laws. We have become dependent on the Judiciary to tell us how to live freely. The idea that we would leave the parameters of freedom in the hands of democratic control has come to be seen as the precursor of despotism. This shows the key success of the human rights industry: to sew deep distrust of the virtue of democracy. This has always been the purpose of human rights law. Its primary purpose has always been to provide a moral justification for transnational government. It was used by Conservative elites in the aftermath of the war to justify the creation of European institutions which were designed to sidestep the influence of national populaces.

Yet what human rights supporters forget, or choose to ignore, is that democracy has been the greatest defender of minority rights that history has ever known. The civil rights movement, the gay rights movement, the free speech movement have all had one thing in common: people. Ordinary members of the public. The association of groups of people, together, working to change public opinion has been the greatest force for change in all of world history. The slander of democracy by the human rights lobby has always been historically illiterate.

What are the consequences for deferring to the Judiciary on matters of freedom? Firstly, we become less free. History has shown us that deference to Judges to secure freedom is utterly futile. Under the reign of the human rights act, the government has been able to extend detention without charge, to further expand our framework of anti-terror laws, to introduce fundamentally draconian policies under the Prevent agenda. Even the most pro-freedom judgements of the UK House of Lords or the European Court of Human Rights promote a deeply qualified and vulnerable idea of freedom.

But, arguably worse than this, in believing in human rights laws, we delegate more responsibility for managing political issues to people who are unelected. Whether Judges are here or on the continent, they are not subject to our democratic control. That is why their remit over politics should be as narrow as possible. Of course there will be difficult cases. Of course, many of the arguments about the undemocratic nature of the European Court of Human Rights are overblown. But their substance is correct. The extent of our political freedom should be determined by those who are electable. Our ideas about freedom should be shaped by us, through popular pressure and agitation. It is only in this relationship that freedom remains, in some meaningful sense, a matter of public contestation.

What is freedom?

In concluding, I'll give you an insight into my writing process. I sent this manuscript out to a few trusted friends to offer some thoughts. They came back with a common remark. This was to ask 'what do you mean by freedom?' The criticism was that I had not set out in detail what I took freedom to consist in.

It struck me that this question rather underlies much of the discussion around human rights. People are asking for someone to tell them how to be free. They are reaching for someone to tell them what 'freedom' means. They are looking for clean definitions that will obviate the need to think clearly about the difficult cases. The balance between freedom of expression and our private lives is a complex social and political question. Isn't it nice that we have a series of judgements by unelected members of the judiciary to tell us where the balance lies?

But freedom is not something anyone can tell you how to

do. In 1900, a Judge would have told you that freedom did not extend to women having the vote. In 1989, a Judge would have told you that freedom did not extend to homosexual activity being allowed in public. Freedom is what we make it. History has taught us again and again that we cannot rely on the law to tell us what freedom looks like.

The problem we face now is that fighting for genuine freedom has come to be seen as threatening. The students we see on college and University campuses calling for clampdowns on freedom are scared of being free. Free speech is equated with violence. Freedom of conscience is equated with bigotry. When these two fundamental political freedoms have become so slandered, it is not surprising that students look for safety and comfort in the form of greater regulation.

The Human Rights Act is not the be all and end all in our discussion on political freedom. There are human rights supporters that will say I have undersold the utility of human rights laws. There will be human rights detractors who will say I have underestimated the negative impact of human rights jurisprudence. However, to focus on the practical use of these laws is to ignore what the public debate around human rights tells us about contemporary society. The panic around the repeal of the human rights act has revealed a profound discomfort with the idea of being free. Repealing the human rights act, and rolling back the roll of judiciary in adjudicating our freedom would not transform our society into a totalitarian state. It may well place the meaning of important freedoms back on the table for public debate.

Endnotes

1. A promise to repeal the Act appeared in the Conservative's 2005 manifesto, with a plan to replace it with a British Bill of Rights, which would only challenge (at most) the supra-national dimension of human rights law.

2. Reporting of the case appeared online at http://www.bbc.co.uk/news/uk-england-derbyshire-38426961

3. See *Britain's Gulag: the Brutal End of the Empire in Kenya* Elkins K Pimlico 2005

4. See Ewing K *Bonfire of the Liberties: New Labour Human Rights and the Rule of Law* Oxford University Press 2010

5. See for example, Hopgood, S *Brexit and Human Rights: Winter is Coming* Open Democracy 2016

6. Sands, P Elson Ethics Lecture 20.10.2015

7. R v A [2001] H.R.L.R. 48

8. See Lord Irvine's speech to the UCL Constitutional Society

9. 2003 Starmer, K European Law Review

10. *The Politics of the Judiciary* Griffith JG

11. *The New Judiciary: the effects of Expansion and Activism* Malleson K, Ashgate Publishing 1999

12. See The *European Court of Human Rights Between Law and Politics* Christoffersen and Madsden, Oxford University Press 2013

13. *The Conservative Human Rights Revolution: European Identity, Transnational Politics and the Origins of the European Convention* Duranti, M OUP USA, 2017

14. See *Postwar: A history of Europe since 1945* T Judt Vintage 2010

15. See eg: the collection of essays archived at Bright Blue: https://humanrights.brightblue.org.uk/publications

16. The campaign is still archived at https://www.indiegogo.com/projects/fighting-hate-with-human-rights

17. See Malleson K as above.

18. See *End of the Party* by Rawnsley, A on Blair's personal loathing of the Act

19. https://www.theguardian.com/politics/2006/may/14/humanrights.ukcrime

20. Fitzpatrick, M and Marshall K *Who Needs the Labour Party?* Junius Publications 1978

21. Ibid.

22. Richard Dimbleby Lecture, BBC 1976

23. See Irvine, K speech to UCL Constitutional Unit Lecture, December 1998. Archived here: https://www.ucl.ac.uk/political-science/publications/unit-publications/35.pdf

24. See eg Gearty and Ewing *The Struggle for Civil Liberties: Political Freedom and the Rule of Law in Britain 1914 – 1945* Oxford University Press

25. A copy is archived online at https://www.conservatives.com/~/media/Files/Manifesto2010

26. http://www.telegraph.co.uk/news/politics/8317257/Nick-Clegg-were-restoring-hard-won-British-liberties.html

27. Speech Cameron D 7th May 2010 The speech is available here: http://www.dailyrecord.co.uk/news/politics/election-2010-david-camerons-speech-1058385

28. http://www.inquirelive.co.uk/opinion/misc/media-and-the-woolwich-attack-why-we-should-be-wary-of-viral-terrorism/

29. https://www.theguardian.com/uk/2013/may/23/woolwich-nick-clegg-communications-bill-risk

30. http://www.independent.co.uk/news/uk/crime/theresa-may-keen-to-revive-snoopers-charter-in-wake-of-woolwich-attack-8629990.html

31. http://www.politics.co.uk/news/2013/05/30/clegg-starts-to-u-turn-on-snoopers-charter-some-bits-of-bill

32. *Brevan Howard Asset Management LLP v (1) Reuters Ltd (2) Maiya Keidan (3) Person or Persons Unknown* [2017] EWCA

Civ 950

33. See *Human Rights and the Uses of History* Moyn S, Verso books 2017

34. https://www.bbc.co.uk/education/topics/z26pb9q/resources/1

35. See the government's White paper: Rights Brought Home, archived here: https://www.gov.uk/government/uploads/system/uploads/attachment_data/file/263526/rights.pdf

36. https://www.theguardian.com/humanrightsandwrongs/800-years-making

37. The video is still available at https://www.theguardian.com/culture/video/2016/apr/25/patrick-stewart-sketch-what-has-the-echr-ever-done-for-us-video

38. Ishay, M University of California Press June 2008

39. Hunt, L W. W. Norton & Company 25 April 2008

40. Gearty C *Human rights: The necessary quest for foundations* January 2012

41. Ibid Moyn S

42. Arendt H *The Origins of Totalitarianism*

43. Arendt H *The Human Condition* University of Chicago Press 1957

44. https://www.liberty-human-rights.org.uk/campaigning/save-our-human-rights-act-0

45. (Application no. 821/03).

46. A review of the circumstances surrounding the deaths of four soldiers at Princess Royal Barracks, Deepcut between 1995 and 2002 by Nicholas Blake QC

47. Ibid para 1.6

48. Ibid

49. Liberty Press Release, July 2014 https://www.liberty-human-rights.org.uk/news/press-releases/new-inquest-ordered-deepcut-death

50. https://www.theguardian.com/uk-news/2016/feb/01/deepcut-inquest-culture-of-sexual-abuse-cheryl-james

51. http://www.inquest.org.uk/statistics/deaths-in-police-custody

52. Her Majesty's Inspectorate of Constabulary and Fire and Rescue Services, October 2017

53. Recent cases include:

54. Report The circumstances surrounding the arrest and prosecution of leading Yukos executives Doc. 10368 29 November 2004

55. https://www.khodorkovsky.com/resources/leutheusser-schnarrenberger-sabine-2/

56. https://www.amnesty.org.uk/press-releases/russia-khodorkovsky-and-lebedev-are-prisoners-conscience

57. https://www.khodorkovsky.com/khodorkovsky-imprisonment-highlighted-in-british-parliament/

58. See eg Sufi and Elmi v the UK in which the applicants demonstrated a real risk from al-Shabaab were they to be deported to Somalia.

59. Of the 10 judgements cited by European Court of Human Rights reports into the UK, 6 found no violation of any provision of the Convention. This of course does not include the vast number of cases that were dismissed by the Court before reaching a judgement.

60. See Sufi and Elmi as cited above

61. *A and Ors v Secretary of State for the Home Department* 2004 UKHL 56

62. *Human Rights and Social Movements* Stammers N Pluto Press 2009

63. Chahal v United Kingdom 15th November 1996; see also *Gebremedhin [Gaberamadhien] v. France*, no. 25389/05, § 74, ECHR 2007-II

64. See coverage of Sher and Others v UK: https://www.theguardian.com/uk-news/2015/oct/20/european-court-human-rights-rules-secret-hearings-legal

65. A phrase adopted by Costas Douzanis in *The End of Human*

Rights Hart Publishing 2000

66. *Why are Millenials wary of Freedom* article by Gary Matter in The New York Times, October 2017

67. Ibid

68. See Spiked's Free Speech University Rankings in which 63.5% of institutions implemented at least some control over what could be said on campus.

69. *The Economist* https://www.economist.com/news/internat ional/21699905-university-protesters-believe-they-are-fighting-justice-their-critics-think-free

Zero Books

CULTURE, SOCIETY & POLITICS

Contemporary culture has eliminated the concept and public figure of the intellectual. A cretinous anti-intellectualism presides, cheer-led by hacks in the pay of multinational corporations who reassure their bored readers that there is no need to rouse themselves from their stupor. Zer0 Books knows that another kind of discourse – intellectual without being academic, popular without being populist – is not only possible: it is already flourishing. Zer0 is convinced that in the unthinking, blandly consensual culture in which we live, critical and engaged theoretical reflection is more important than ever before.

If you have enjoyed this book, why not tell other readers by posting a review on your preferred book site.

Recent bestsellers from Zero Books are:

In the Dust of This Planet
Horror of Philosophy vol. 1
Eugene Thacker
In the first of a series of three books on the Horror of
Philosophy, *In the Dust of This Planet* offers the genre of horror
as a way of thinking about the unthinkable.
Paperback: 978-1-84694-676-9 ebook: 978-1-78099-010-1

Capitalist Realism
Is there no alternative?
Mark Fisher
An analysis of the ways in which capitalism has presented itself
as the only realistic political-economic system.
Paperback: 978-1-84694-317-1 ebook: 978-1-78099-734-6

Rebel Rebel
Chris O'Leary
David Bowie: every single song. Everything you want to know,
everything you didn't know.
Paperback: 978-1-78099-244-0 ebook: 978-1-78099-713-1

Cartographies of the Absolute
Alberto Toscano, Jeff Kinkle
An aesthetics of the economy for the twenty-first century.
Paperback: 978-1-78099-275-4 ebook: 978-1-78279-973-3

Malign Velocities
Accelerationism and Capitalism
Benjamin Noys
Long listed for the Bread and Roses Prize 2015, *Malign Velocities* argues against the need for speed, tracking acceleration as the symptom of the ongoing crises of capitalism.
Paperback: 978-1-78279-300-7 ebook: 978-1-78279-299-4

Meat Market
Female Flesh under Capitalism
Laurie Penny
A feminist dissection of women's bodies as the fleshy fulcrum of capitalist cannibalism, whereby women are both consumers and consumed.
Paperback: 978-1-84694-521-2 ebook: 978-1-84694-782-7

Poor but Sexy
Culture Clashes in Europe East and West
Agata Pyzik
How the East stayed East and the West stayed West.
Paperback: 978-1-78099-394-2 ebook: 978-1-78099-395-9

Romeo and Juliet in Palestine
Teaching Under Occupation
Tom Sperlinger
Life in the West Bank, the nature of pedagogy and the role of a university under occupation.
Paperback: 978-1-78279-637-4 ebook: 978-1-78279-636-7

Sweetening the Pill
or How we Got Hooked on Hormonal Birth Control
Holly Grigg-Spall
Has contraception liberated or oppressed women? *Sweetening the Pill* breaks the silence on the dark side of hormonal contraception.
Paperback: 978-1-78099-607-3 ebook: 978-1-78099-608-0

Why Are We The Good Guys?
Reclaiming your Mind from the Delusions of Propaganda
David Cromwell
A provocative challenge to the standard ideology that Western power is a benevolent force in the world.
Paperback: 978-1-78099-365-2 ebook: 978-1-78099-366-9

Readers of ebooks can buy or view any of these bestsellers by clicking on the live link in the title. Most titles are published in paperback and as an ebook. Paperbacks are available in traditional bookshops. Both print and ebook formats are available online.

Find more titles and sign up to our readers' newsletter at http://www.johnhuntpublishing.com/culture-and-politics

Follow us on Facebook at https://www.facebook.com/ZeroBooks

and Twitter at https://twitter.com/Zer0Books